Journey Every Step Un-Sure

Journey Every Step Un-Sure

Vincent N. Scialo

authorHOUSE®

AuthorHouse™
1663 Liberty Drive
Bloomington, IN 47403
www.authorhouse.com
Phone: 1-800-839-8640

First published by AuthorHouse   04/14/2011

ISBN: 978-1-4567-6911-6 (sc)
ISBN: 978-1-4567-6910-9 (ebk)

Printed in the United States of America

Any people depicted in stock imagery provided by Thinkstock are models, and such images are being used for illustrative purposes only.

Certain stock imagery © Thinkstock.

This book is printed on acid-free paper.

Also by Vincent N. Scialo

The Rocking Chair
Randolph's Tale (A Journey for Love)
Deep in the Woods
Heigh-Ho
Not By Choice

Dedication

Jen, my wife, my life, my friend. Always and forever.
Marissa, my daughter, my life, my friend. Now and forever.
Jeff, my son, my life, my friend, to Infinity and beyond.
You all complete me and make me who I am. Ocean, sky, world, sea! The Scialo Power of four for me!

To all my family and friends who have impacted me in positive ways throughout my life, I give you thanks. You all know who you are and there aren't enough words to express my gratitude.

And lastly, to the greatest gift of all. **JESUS**. For without you, none of this would be possible.

God Bless and Thanks.

1

Did you ever wake up in the dead of the night or at early morning light and ask yourself this one simple question, "Why am I here?" Or, "What is my real purpose in life?" Or even, "Why do I exist?" Whether it be a workday, or a more leisurely day, did you ever stop and ponder the most profound question of all: "Why was I born?" I know I have many times more than I care to remember. What I am about to share with you is the story of my life and how these questions came to be answered, believed and ultimately cherished. Some of you will embrace my revelations while others will be skeptical. Those of you who doubt will be known as my Thomas as it will take much convincing with probable cause or facts. Once my message is fully received and welcomed, the rewards will overcome the doubts. What I witnessed and experienced will make each and every person a better individual. Not only for others to see, but deep down within the spirit of your soul. My experience of this journey that I share shall enlighten you. The rest of my tale after that will fall into a place like no other. Beyond your wildest imagination. To a belief from birth, we all long for.

2

I ask myself this question time and time again, "Why me? Why was I put on this planet we call Earth?" In retrospect I come up with many different scenarios. After much consideration and deep thought I usually sate my spiritual appetite with the following considerations. You see, every person does indeed have a meaningful purpose to his or her existence. You may not possess physical beauty, stature, or intelligence which sets you apart from the ordinary. You may not possess the wealth which makes others envy your financial status, but your spirit can be enriched beyond your wildest imaginings. My goal is to share with you insights of greater importance. Open your mind, your heart, and most importantly your beliefs and get ready to believe like you never believed before. My name is Jack Rogan Reilly and this is my story.

3

It was just another ordinary Wednesday afternoon that I entered this world. The birth records state my full name as Jack Rogan Reilly. I would remain an only child born to Maeve Ohara-Reilly and Seamus Reilly on April 11th 1928, weighing seven pounds, eleven ounces. Because of complications, which almost cost my mother her life during delivery, doctors told her that any future pregnancies would be unwise. My father, a practical man, felt that to endanger his one and only treasure, my mother, would be too much of a risk for the sake of a large family. Seamus was pleased with a son, who would carry on the family name, and legacy following in his footsteps. You see my father was a very wealthy self-made man. My parents met in Ireland coming from their hometown on the outskirts of Dublin. Both of them had very large families, where food was scare and barely enough to feed them. Seamus worked hard on the family farm and longed for the one opportunity where he could come to America, the land of golden opportunity. Rumors among villagers of a better place to live called

America, always caught his interest and the burning desire to leave poverty for a better life tormented Seamus. He diligently strived to one day leave behind all he didn't have for a chance to better himself. When he finally met his soon to be wife Maeve, at a Church dance, it was love at first sight. Maeve, too, having come from a large poor family had the same desires as her soon to be husband. Together they scrimped and saved every pence they could muster for the chance of a lifetime. Having met when they were both only fourteen years old, it took several years before they could afford the expense of two steerage class one-way tickets to America. After marrying in their small hometown at eighteen, and saying their heart-wrenching farewells to families and friends who would never be forgotten, they dried their tears, and opened their eyes to a bright new future.

4

Having come to America in the early 1920's, Seamus set out to make his fortune. Crossing over the Atlantic Ocean and seeing the Statue of Liberty as the ship sailed past, gave him all the confidence needed, to ensure he would succeed in this great country called America. After passing through customs at Ellis Island and with no real plan as to where they would settle, Seamus chose Coney Island as their prime residence. With subways that ran to and from Manhattan, the location and proximity suited them perfectly. After exploring the subway maps, Seamus and Maeve took the D train to the last stop in Brooklyn. After getting off the train they proceeded to walk toward the shoreline and gazed with amazement at the Wonder Wheel, which was a Ferris wheel of great proportions. I had been told often as a child that my mother fell in love with the Wonder Wheel and on many occasions, both my parents would ride it frequently. Seamus and Maeve, with their small life savings and one suitcase of personal belongings trudged on in this unfamiliar land of promise. Immediately upon seeing the street sign for Mermaid Ave, Maeve rambled on and on how she would like to live on a street with such a magical name. For centuries mermaids existed as a fantasy existence for little girls. Maeve as a young girl in school often sat listening to her teacher read about the tales of the ocean and all the magical creatures that inhibited the vast domain. Knowing it would be a losing battle to argue their first dwelling being anywhere other than on Mermaid Avenue, they finally came upon a small apartment, on the third floor of a four-story building. It was on 18th Street, just a few short blocks from Stillwell Avenue and the subway line. After settling in and making the apartment a home, Seamus went into the city each and every day in hopes of securing a job. For the first few weeks there was no success in his search for employment. Although he was a farmer back in Ireland, he really had no training or skills in any other fields required for working in New York City. Although Seamus prided himself with his ability to talk to just about anyone, employers were not interested in a young man with a heavy Irish brogue. Frustrated that his dream for financial security was not easily attained, Seamus continued to travel back and forth to Manhattan. Maeve stood by and always encouraged him that opportunity waited just around the corner and to never give up. Jack could picture both his parents in their tiny kitchen discussing their future amidst their dwindling life savings over a hot home cooked meal prepared by his mother.

"Seamus, we shall know better times just lying ahead round the bend. Have faith in yourself," Maeve stated as she placed the pot of stew on the table.

"My sweet Maeve, always the dreamer. How did I get so lucky to win you over?" asked Seamus while he blew on his spoonful of hot stew.

"Perhaps you got lucky cause all the others were taken and I being the prettiest of the lot was available," giggled Maeve.

"Yes, but these New York people are bullocks if you ask me. Not to even give me a chance. I mean I haven't got a baldy why they aren't interested in the likes of me?"

"Don't be so hard on yourself. Away with you and this foolish banter. I would hire you in a flash. A tall dark Irishman like yourself."

"If they aren't lighting up their fags then they are all telling me fibs so they don't have to give me work."

"I am in the wick. You can't be telling me that is how it goes," Maeve replied after pouring them both a glass of milk.

"Whether or not I'm still pulling me plum by just sitting around here day after day."

"Doing nothing is absurd! You try your earnest to find work each and every day. Now stop talking like a caffler."

Seamus slid his chair over to Maeve so that he was right alongside her and gently placed his hand on top of hers, "How about giving me a little shift on the lips?"

Maeve put her hand over his and squeezed it, "Seamus, if I didn't know you better I would say that you were up to shenanigans. And, we haven't even finished this lovely stew I prepared."

"Since I seem to be a failure in finding employment, maybe I could make it up to you in the bedroom."

Maeve gazed at this loving man. She knew she would never have chosen anyone else to spend her life with. To be the father of her children. With his dark hair and blue eyes, he was the envy of most men in their hometown. Tall at almost six feet and built like an athlete, she admired him for the man he truly was. Now as she pushed away her plate and stood from the table, she took him by his other hand, "You know I should give you a shiner for having cooked this stew only to go cold on this table."

Seamus laughed as he let his petite brown-haired, brown-eyed, fair skinned Irish beauty lead him to where he knew pleasure awaited. He hoped the lovemaking would erase all the burdens they were presently facing. Deep down he knew if he couldn't soon find a means to support his one genuine treasure in life, things would soon get troublesome. For now he was grateful for the distraction as he, too, stood and said, "Lead the way my fair maiden, lead the way."

5

As luck would soon have it, Seamus' life was about to change for the better. Approximately three months after Seamus and Maeve first saw Lady Liberty, being in the right place at the right time would prove to be advantageous. Seamus was in route to the 'D' train on Stillwell Avenue and as he walked up 18th street to the corner of Neptune Avenue, he suddenly came to a stop. A couple of local bowery street-fighting boys were picking on a young Jewish boy who wore a Yarmulke. Each boy was taking turns pushing the little boy from kid to kid. The young Jewish boy had dropped his book bag and papers were strewn all over the pavement. The taunting was getting more vicious and Seamus knew that soon it would escalate resulting in the little boy getting hurt. Not even giving time to contemplate the serious consequences with the group of bowery boys who were not much younger than himself, Seamus approached the group. They were continuing to torment the young boy when the leader of the pack noticed him, "Don't you think you should just keep on walking and mind your business for your own good!"

Seamus just glared at the ring leader knowing that if he stared him down, they might leave the young boy alone.

Sensing the lone boy watching him intently and not backing down, the ring leader took a step toward him, "I'm not asking you to move along, I'm telling you to leave NOW!"

Seamus stood his ground after having just been shouted at, "What do you have against this mere young lad? Looks to me like he aint done anything to warrant this abuse."

Now the whole gang stopped and moved a bit closer to him, leaving the young Jewish boy enough time to pick up his belongings and start to back up slowly.

The leader chuckled after hearing the heavy Irish brogue, "So what do we have here. Look boys, a real live Irish Mick. When did you come over? Sounds to me like you just got off the boat."

Knowing it best to answer with a calm and cool voice he responded, "Look boys, I don't want no trouble here. Just leave the boy be and let's say we all call it a day." With their full attention on Seamus, the young Jewish boy darted away so fast that the gang ignored him, and focused their attention to their newest challenge.

Seamus knew he would have to act fast, if he wanted to get out of this with no major cuts or bruises. Without a moment's notice and none too soon, he lunged right smack into the ring leader's stomach, knocking the wind out of him and sending him down on his knees.

After catching the leader off guard and with him down on the ground, he blindly swung his fist to the next guy in the circle, catching him dead square in the chin and sending him flying backwards. The remaining two stood dead in their tracks unable to fight back since they felt they were up against a bully too tough to handle. Seamus knew he had seconds at most to get out of there, so he pushed past the two standing figures, and headed in the same direction that the Jewish boy had fled. When he was just yards away from the subway, he heard a young boy cry out, "That's him papa! That's the boy who saved me."

6

It turned out that the young Jewish boy's father owned a very successful financial company in Manhattan. As a thank you for protecting his son from what he was sure would have been great harm, he offered Seamus a job in his company after hearing that he was in need of employment. This convinced the father, that from some unfortunate incidents, good can truly prevail. The following day Seamus rode the subway with Albert Rothman, to his first day as a helper in the mailroom. Rothman Gold was a very successful brokerage firm, located in the financial district known as Wall Street. Seamus, unknowingly, had just stepped on the first rung of the ladder of success.

7

Days turned into weeks, weeks into months, and eventually years had gone by for Seamus and Maeve. Under the wing of one of the most powerful brokers in Manhattan, Seamus learned the workings of the firm inside and out. Albert Rothman promoted young Seamus, from a mail room apprentice, through every other department within his firm. Starting in the mailroom for minimum wage, and advancing at a fast pace due to the fact he was a very quick learner, benefited the Reilly's. He learned accounting, payroll, office administration and daily trading from the most prestigious of Rothman Gold. Each and every night after dinner, Seamus would read about the stock market, and all the trades of the past day. Eventually, he became the most lucrative trader the firm had. Seamus was treated not like any other employee by Albert, but more like a son. Since Albert's only son, Jeremy, had no interest in learning his father's business and his three daughters were to marry and provide him with grandchildren, Seamus ranked as his right hand man. Jeremy on occasion would visit while he attended college in Manhattan, but showed no jealousy since his main interest in life was to be a pianist. Over the years Jeremy took a liking to Seamus and never forgot the valor that Seamus exhibited that awful day with the bowery boys, so many years ago. After all, Seamus was an asset to his father's firm with a young man's enthusiasm and quest for knowledge and resulting success that was necessary in a growing economy within the country.

8

Maeve was delighted by her husband's success. What could have been a nightmare immigrant experience, their American dream, had proved anything but. Now five years later, Seamus and Maeve still occupied the same apartment building they had when they first arrived in Coney Island.

However, instead of renting the third floor apartment on Mermaid Avenue, they had just recently purchased the four-story building, from the widow, who had just passed away. Seamus immediately moved them down to the first floor and had the entire floor renovated to one living space occupying the main floor. Now with income from six other rentals coming in monthly, money flowed freely. Together they had decided to send money back to their families in Ireland. Time and time again, they tried to persuade their parents and all their siblings to come across the Atlantic to a better life. For reasons they would never know, their offers were always declined. The financial help was much appreciated and acknowledged in correspondence between letters back and forth, but never a mention of leaving to start anew. With no other family but each other, the next best thing was to start their own family.

9

Although the timing was right to begin a brood of their own, Maeve was unable to conceive. After months of trying, frustration was taking its toll on both of them. Seamus wanted nothing more than a son to carry on his name, in this land of fortune. Sensing the disappointment Seamus would feel, Maeve would weep after every month knowing that she was not pregnant. This continued for almost a year and a half before the time came when her period stopped. Elated, delighted and ecstatic were too few of words to describe Seamus' constant mood from that moment on. There weren't enough flowers to buy that he could bring home to his lovely wife. Each day he presented her with a different type of flower. Roses, daisies, lilies, and tulips were just some of the many he gave her. As the flowers bloomed so did Maeve in her pregnancy. Together the Reilly's waited, counted, and crossed out each day, in anticipation of the longed-for little bundle of joy.

10

Finally, the time had come. Seamus had run over to where Albert Rothman lived to inform him that he would need some time off to take Maeve to the hospital. Rushing back to his apartment, he grabbed the previously packed suitcase in one hand, and gently took Maeve by the elbow with the other. Escorting her for the short walk to Coney Island Hospital on Ocean Parkway, he headed in the direction of Neptune Avenue. Once he pushed open the doors and informed the nurses of the pending delivery, Maeve was rushed off to the maternity wing. Seamus was not permitted in that wing of the hospital, so he sat in the waiting area. What felt like an eternity, but in all reality was no more than a couple of hours, turned from a peaceful moment to complete mayhem. Suddenly, two nurses rushed into the waiting room inquiring among the visitors if there was a Mr. Reilly present. Immediately sensing that something had gone terribly wrong from the look of panic on the nurses' faces, he jumped up from his seat. Telling him to follow them, the nurses rushed him to the delivery room, where he saw Maeve. Her face was covered in sweat and her skin looked more ashen than he had ever seen. As he entered the private area, he was taken to the side by a robust but short man who introduced himself as Doctor Morelli. With a quick update of her current condition, and by the appearance of his beloved wife, Seamus knew time was of the essence. Dr. Morelli explained if the baby couldn't be delivered in the next ten minutes, and in order to save both mother and child, the doctor needed to perform an emergency Cesarean delivery. Relying on this brief explanation and with no medical knowledge, Seamus signed the hospital paperwork giving permission to proceed further. Asked to once again wait outside the delivery area, Seamus went to the hospital chapel to pray to a God he knew wouldn't let him down.

11

Seamus knelt at the altar for what felt like a lifetime. Praying, bargaining, and even offering himself in place of Maeve, time slowly ticked by. When he finally felt strong enough to leave the chapel, and head in the direction of what he hoped was anything but gloom, he left behind his present source of strength. A God like no other. Scared and frightened of what news may lie ahead, he tiptoed down the hall. Determined not to collapse by what he may have to endure, Seamus saw Doctor Morelli exiting the delivery room.

"Doctor Morelli. Doctor, is she okay. Please . . . . is Maeve okay?" came from a trembling voice.

"Mr. Reilly. It was very touch and go for a while in there. We almost weren't able to stop your wife's bleeding, but . . ." the doctor was interrupted mid-sentence.

"Oh, Lord. We made a deal. You promised me. Oh God you promised," pleaded Seamus into thin air.

"Mr. Reilly, Mr. Reilly, please calm down. Have a seat." Doctor Morelli realized that there would be no other way but the direct way to finish this conversation. This new father was going to faint if the good news wasn't given faster. The father's flat expressionless face just staring ahead said it all.

"Listen to me, Mr. Reilly. Both your wife and son are doing fine. We were able to stop the bleeding, but we were required to perform the procedure we explained to you before. My only concern is that going forward you cannot jeopardize your wife by having any more children. Her insides, unfortunately, are not strong enough for carrying babies. Internally she is too weak," Seamus was listening, but once he heard his Maeve and son were doing fine, the rest was a blur. Later, both he and Maeve could sit down with this wonderful doctor and go over all the details. Right now, all he wanted was to see his beautiful Maeve and new baby boy. Gaining back his confidence, he started to babble like a proud new father, "Did you say both of them were doing fine? Did I hear you correctly? Oh, thank you God! Thank you Blessed Mother! Thank you Jesus and all the Saints in Heaven. Blessed be you all!"

And just like that, Doctor Morelli led the way for Seamus to see his adored wife and the biggest accomplishment yet in his life. The arrival of their new son. The future Jack Rogan Reilly.

12

There is no greater love for a child, than a parent's love, and Jack was showered with it.

Realizing that this was to be their only child, both Maeve and Seamus spoiled their most precious boy. As their infant son grew bigger each week, Seamus, who would work late hours at the office, now rushed home to be with him. Maeve was thrilled to have her husband share in the daily chores that involved Jack. Bathing, changing and feeding him brought joy to her husband and delighted her beyond words. As little Jack learned to sit up, crawl and entertain them with something new each day, they constantly doted on him. With red-hair, blue eyes and fair skin like his mother, he was a classic Irish baby. Choosing Rogan, which means red, as his middle name, they found it ironic that his hair grew redder as it filled in. Seamus resorted to calling him JR, simply because he liked the initials of both his names. So after a while both mother and father, would refer to him as JR in their daily conversations, while talking about him. JR was a fast learner, as he proved to be, when he started to walk just before his first birthday in late March of 1929. Delighted and thrilled by his first steps and in celebration of his first birthday, they took young JR to Coney Island Amusement Park for the first of many more visits to follow.

13

It was early May, when Maeve and Seamus were able to take JR to Coney Island. Seamus was busier than ever at the brokerage firm now and trading was at an all-time high the last several weeks. Economists were concerned about global trading and the impact it could have on the United States. Many nights, Seamus was too tired from a day at the office, that he would skip dinner, just to spend a bit of time with his son, before the exhaustion overtook him. Today, Seamus and Maeve promised each other a full weekend day at the amusement park with no talk of business. The stress of the workload was etched on Seamus' face over the past few weeks. A day at Coney Island was much needed, as was the quality time with his wife and son.

Peering off into the distance as they walked to the park Seamus spoke, "What do you say we ride the Ferris Wheel first. Then we can dander along the boardwalk."

"It's called the Wonder Wheel. I've watched it once, when I took JR for an early morning stroll. Some of the cars roll inside some type of track while the remaining others stay stationary on the outside. Kinda scary if you ask me. But if it means you spending time on the doss, then I say we make a go of it."

"Me, goof off. Why never Mrs. Reilly. Mother of our son. Do I look to you like I waste time," laughed Seamus, as he took JR up into his arms and kissed him lovingly on the cheek.

Seamus walked up to the booth and paid for the Wonder Wheel tickets.

Together, they stood in line and waited for their turn to board a car. Standing under the giant wheel made it all the more enormous to the eye. Maeve's heart started to race and she thought it would never stop racing. She felt exhilarated although confused, delighted but frightened, riddled with disbelief that they would soon be riding on top of the world. Gazing up she was amazed, astonished, eager but wary, cautious and as close to scared, as she had ever been. Noticing his wife looking up, down and back again, he asked, "You are sure you want to ride this my fair maiden? Looks to me like you been having some second doubts."

"No, yes, oh, I don't really know. I mean Seamus, look at how huge this contraption is. What if it should break down with us at the top. I mean how in all of heaven's earth do we get down?"

Holding back an urge to laugh, he comforted and reassured her, "Do you think I would let something happen to you? I'm sure this has been operating for a donkey's years if not longer. If this thing should fail on us, I'll be the first to carry you and my cub JR down pole by pole. Now relax, nothing is going to happen to us. Just think of the breathtaking view we'll have if we do get stuck up top."

"Honestly, Seamus. You know all the right things to put my nerves back in check. I know I'll enjoy this first time experience especially with both my men with me."

As the line shortened and they were next for a car, Seamus reached over when it stopped in front of them. Opening the small door to let them in, Seamus took a bow and held his hand out, "Your chariot awaits you, m'lady!"

After getting in one of the stationary cars, the wheel circled around for a full three revolutions.

Looking in one direction they could see all of Coney Island, from the homes along the avenues to the subway line and beyond. If they looked in the other direction they saw the boardwalk with all the shops and rides. And with a gentle breeze off the ocean, in that direction they could see an ocean wider than their eyes could scan. Breathtaking, enchanted and even mesmerizing were words Maeve used to describe their first ride. She even begged Seamus to go on it again, but to try the cars that rode the inner tracks. No longer frightened, she wanted to ride it over and over again. Seamus promised they would before the day's end, but first headed for Nathan's, which he had been told had the world's best hot dogs and French fries on all of the eastern sea coast. So after lunch, which indeed lived up to their expectations, and some rides suited more for JR, they once again rode the Wonder Wheel. Walking along the boardwalk, Seamus promised Maeve they would do this more often when possible, which left Maeve smiling cheek to cheek. After a long day at the Coney Island Amusements, they headed home. Maeve, in total wonder, at what was a truly beautiful day and Seamus, in awe, of the quality time spent with his family. Both of them, were unaware just how all that was about to change for the worse, in just a few short months.

14

As fast as spring arrived, summer came even faster. Maeve and Seamus were able to spend at least one day of the weekend at the amusement park. Coney Island was crowded with beach revelers, as well as others who enjoyed the boardwalk and rides. Sweltering temperatures led most people down to the ocean, where a cool breeze could be found. At times, record crowds would visit both the beach and boardwalk. This still didn't stop the Reilly's. With no shortage of cash, they enjoyed every ride and food concession available. The Wonder Wheel was, of course, their favorite among all the others. The other rides were good too. The Cyclone stood alone and was noted as one of the best wooden roller coasters in the world. Since it had opened in 1927, for two years now, the line for the Cyclone would stretch out blocks on any given day. Even the Whip, Tip Top, and Tilt-a-Whirl were popular among the riders. Of the smaller rides, the Caterpillar made little JR chuckle the most. As the summer came to an end and with Labor Day approaching, Seamus needed to spend more time than usual at the brokerage firm of Rothman Gold. Trading was out of control and on September 3rd, the day after Labor Day, the stock market closed with the Dow at an all-time pre-crash high of 381.17. It wouldn't reach that mark again for twenty-five years. The following day there was an immediate fall in stock prices worrying all economists and traders. Seamus wasn't himself and Maeve was concerned that the ups and downs of this business he was in, would one day get the best of him. The next couple of weeks were a roller coaster ride. Not realizing just how crazy the nation would soon become, October 24th, known as Black Thursday, began. The Stock Market crash had begun. Panic selling was triggered by predictions of the impending crash. Five top banks put up about 20 million each to buy stock and to restore confidence in the market. It seemed to work. There was a late rally, and the Dow closed at 299.47 with a record 13 million shares traded. Seamus was spending more hours at the office than ever, with barely any sleep at all. Maeve would pack him a sandwich for lunch, along with something for dinner, knowing he would be gone the whole day. Her concerns for her husband continued, and the strain on his well-being was unbearable for her. She, too, was losing sleep over the current economic status of the country. Only four days later the panic selling resumed. The Dow dropped almost 40 points which was nearly 13 percent and previously unheard of.

What was soon to be noted as the worst day in American financial history, along came Black Tuesday, October 29th. The Dow dropped another 30 points to close at 230.07 with the trading of 16 million shares. It was official news throughout the nation. The stock market had crashed. The comfortable life the Reilly's had become accustomed to was about to change.

15

The next few months, the floor of the country had fallen out from under everyone's feet. The unemployment rate continued to soar, with millions losing their jobs because companies were folding. Never had a nation as strong as the United States been impacted so drastically. Many companies trading on the stock market closed their doors and brokerage firms too. The wealthy were hit the hardest, since most of their fortunes were invested in stocks and bonds. Even banks couldn't pay their customers, who wanted to withdraw their money just to get by. The country was out of control. Businessmen were committing suicide at unbelievable rates over the loss of their fortunes. A total frenzy was happening that could not be slowed, stopped or even prevented. The once proud nation of the free and the brave was collapsing. The entire world's economy was also affected. Things were as bad as they could get. That is what the Reilly's wanted to believe.

16

Seamus was beyond despair. He had witnessed more destruction and devastation then he ever thought imaginable. It wasn't until six months later that his worse nightmare would begin. Albert Rothman's brokerage firm was hit hard. Most of their securities from banks were lost. Having no where to turn for financial support and with four children of his own, his fortune dwindled at a fast rate. Unable to bounce back with any type of monetary gain in his personal assets, Albert, like so many others before him, rode the elevator to the top floor of the building in Manhattan. It was early morning and most of his remaining staff hadn't arrived to work. Albert left a lengthy note apologizing mostly to his wife and children for what he felt was his only way out. Always the provider and with the elegant life style he had for so many years lived, this, in his eyes, was his one–way ticket out. Seamus and two other employees would find Albert's letter addressed to his wife, just a few short minutes too late. On a crystal clear Thursday morning, while the early birds were in search of the worms, Albert jumped off the ledge of the roof to soar high above the clouds. But instead of flying among the other birds, Albert raced at a deadly speed straight toward the pavement.

17

Upon reading the last words put to paper by Albert, Seamus was in total shock. Never in his life would he expect his boss and friend to resort to such drastic measures. Sooner or later things would have to improve. You only had to wait out the storm for the skies to turn blue again. Seamus wished he had arrived earlier to see certain signs of dismay on Mr. Rothman's face. Seamus knew for years to come, he would agonize over the fact that he just may have prevented this tragedy from occurring, if only he saw the signs. Ironically enough, time wasn't willing to wait regarding his future either.

18

After the burial and week-long services for his dear beloved friend and employer, Seamus was officially out of work. Rothman Gold had closed its doors like so many businesses in the same situation. Maeve knew this would be a blow to her husband, who in return could suffer great setbacks. As in the last few weeks, two out of their four tenants, had left their building to move in with other relatives, during what was now known as the Great Depression. The other two families had pleaded with Seamus to let them stay in their apartments just a little while longer, in hopes of finding employment enabling them to pay their rents. Seamus, being the saintly man that he was, agreed, knowing full well that times were tough for everyone. With the strain and constant burden to find work of his own, the weight of the world was on his shoulders too. Days went by and weeks as well and eventually the months flew by as well. There were no opportunities available for any type of work. Seamus resorted to selling some of their treasured personal belongings to provide some much needed cash. He even allowed the two tenants to remain rent free, knowing they were in the same boat. Seamus had even resorted to listing his building for sale since investors were few and far between and there was no interest shown. Then on a Sunday morning as he, Maeve and his dearest child left church services, Seamus felt pain within his chest. Not willing to alarm his dearest wife, he kept it to himself. As he sat down to dinner hours later, and ate Maeve's wonderful and famous Irish stew, Seamus excused himself and went to the bedroom to rest. Maeve who at this point was very concerned, but fearful of upsetting her husband, let him be. It wouldn't be until the stroke of midnight that Maeve would lean over to kiss him goodnight, that her lips would fall upon the cold skin of his forehead. Hours later, she would be informed that her cherished husband had perished in his sleep from a massive heart attack.

19

Not having any family to help her with the funeral arrangements, Maeve now faced her grief alone. Writing home to her family comforted her, but at the same didn't provide her with the emotional support she needed. Deep down she knew that neither side of their families would journey to the states to help her get through it. Alone, frightened, and very much isolated, Maeve did her best to plan a decent burial for the man she was supposed to grow old with. Mr. and Mrs. Wilkenson, one of the two tenants who still lived in the upstairs apartment, helped to care for young JR while she planned the funeral. Sadly enough JR was turning two the day of the actual church service. Maeve used what little money they had left to cover the costs of his burial and the grave plot. The next week was a blur to poor Maeve who quietly grieved among people who were mostly strangers to her. They offered only kind words about Seamus. When the mass at Our Lady of Solace, located just blocks away was over, they proceeded to Seamus' final resting place, Green-Wood Cemetery. With little JR dressed in his Sunday best at her side, Maeve knelt down and gently placed a rose on her husband's casket. Two men from the brokerage firm, whom she remembered Seamus talking about as friends, helped her to her feet. Afterwards, about twenty or so people went back to her home for refreshments and to say their last goodbyes. Some of the local neighbors who could still afford to cook extra food, brought over a dish. As the day gave way to night and the last guest had paid their respects, Maeve took little JR in her arms. That night Maeve dreamt of a long life of only happy times with Seamus and tiny Jack. Unfortunately, she was unaware of how short life really was.

20

Struggling to just get by and with no improvement in the current economic state of the country, Maeve was totally distraught. Her finances were scarce and just putting food on the table for her and her child was becoming difficult. Maeve struggled daily with how she would feed her child. Many people faced starvation and she, like many others, waited on long lines for milk and bread. Many times on their way home, Maeve watched others stare at her with the intent to take what little she was given to eat. Often, she would go with Mr. Wilkenson to the food line just for the safety of not being robbed of her precious food. On a cold November day just months after her husband's passing, Maeve thought she was finally free of her financial struggles. An investor, who came smartly dressed in full business attire, was interested in buying their apartment building and made her a very lucrative offer that she couldn't refuse. For the next three weeks the so called gentleman showed genuine interest for the well-being of Maeve and JR. On some occasions, he even brought her food that she hadn't been able to buy for herself. Foods that she tasted when times were good in life, but now craved from her new level of poverty. Without pressuring her and by befriending her in a very vulnerable time in her life, he persuaded her to make the right decision. Not having an attorney that she could afford to represent her in the closing of the building, Maeve read and signed all the papers alone. What Maeve didn't understand was the fine print of the contractual arrangement and what the terms of the agreement clearly stated. So after the deal was finalized, Maeve was given a small token of cash as full payment. Unknowingly Maeve was blindsided by a small time crook, who took advantage of a very young widow, and stole her property for next to nothing. To make matters even worse, the contract stipulated that she would be given ninety days to find a new residence or she would face eviction from the only place she had ever known as home in America.

21

Ninety days had come and gone in a flash and Maeve was left homeless.

The meager amount of money from the sale of her building by a thief, who took all the right measures in ripping her off, was spent. Having no place to turn, she went to the only place she knew to seek refuge; Our Lady of Solace church which was known among the immigrants population. Father Bill Cooligan was the residing pastor of the church and had presided over Seamus' funeral months prior. After pleading and explaining her dire circumstances to Father Bill about her current situation, and having nowhere else to go, he allowed her to spend the night, while he promised to make other arrangements for her and JR. Father Bill, a priest at the parish for twelve years, was a portly man in his late forties. Standing at five foot seven with salt and pepper hair, Father Bill was known as a very compassionate priest in the tiny community. Realizing that a young woman and child left homeless in the streets would be extremely dangerous, he allowed her to stay in the church overnight. He wouldn't be able to live with himself if something were to happen to them because he had sent them on their way. Most others who pleaded and told their stories to Father Bill didn't affect him the way that Maeve and her little boy had. The others were families with fathers who could somehow manage to find some sort of means to get by. In any case, his church couldn't take in large families. Even the churches had been hit hard due to the Great Depression with next to no tithing in the Sunday collections. The next day when Maeve and JR were gathering their small belongings to leave the parish, Father Bill told them to stay at the church until he could find her some suitable place to live. Grateful for a place to live in these difficult times, Maeve resorted to doing all the chores required by Father Bill. Cooking, cleaning, ironing were just a few of the daily requirements for the life of a priest. Since the church was relatively small, there were only three assigned nuns, who however, were elderly and unable to assist in these mundane household tasks. Maeve took charge as if she had worked there for years. Father Bill was so pleased with her eagerness to assist that he went to the Diocese of Brooklyn and spoke on her behalf. Monsignor John Harding IV was presented such a case in Maeve's defense that he, too, relinquished to Father Bill's request. Maeve and her only son would be permitted to live at the rectory as the official housekeeper and cook with a minimum monthly allowance to subsidize her workload. Food would have to be rationed to accommodate two more mouths to feed. Maeve was so grateful to Father Bill and believed that her faith in the Lord above, also played a role in her salvation. A salvation to live on despite all the poverty that surrounded her.

22

Life with Father Bill was, at times, not what she anticipated. The work was continuous and Maeve spent long hours keeping up with what was needed to be done. Three parishes had closed over the course of the first few years of the depression, and many older priests and nuns had come to live at Our Lady of Solace. As the only cook and housekeeper, her day started at dawn and ended well after sunset each evening. Pleased that she had a roof over her head, Maeve never complained. The fact that she and JR had food in their bellies, was enough compared to the circumstances of so many others. With a full parish now requiring additional food, Maeve would often pass on an occasional meal to give more to JR. She made a vow to herself to do whatever it would take, to keep her and her joy nourished and with a bed to sleep in. Given that mother and child shared a bed, only cemented their bond more. As JR grew from a toddler to a small boy and now a young grade school boy, Maeve was proud of him. Now faced with his schooling, along with her limited means to provide transportation, his ability to even attend was a concern. Father Bill once again stepped forward to ensure her son would get a proper education. Indebted to this spiritual man forever, Maeve worshipped a God, she knew had saved her life by sending Father Bill to her in a time of need.

23

JR had become an excellent student and loved numbers. Each teacher he had from grade to grade took notice of his love for numbers, and on more than one occasion brought this to Maeve's attention. Undeniably, JR would add, subtract, multiply and divide in a fraction of the time it took his other classmates. Sure to be precise and accurate at most calculations, JR surprised most teachers with this hidden ability. To compensate or more often reward him for his efforts, Maeve would save the little she earned to take them to Coney Island amusement park. Over time as he grew older, Maeve would allow him to visit the pier by himself, since many memories of her life with Seamus there brought tears to her eyes. So as a mature ten year old, JR would spend endless hours on the weekend visiting the boardwalk alone. Even without money, JR would hang out mostly by himself, since he preferred it that way, along the world's famous boardwalk. Usually he would ride the Wonder Wheel whenever possible, since his mother had shared their love for it as a family, when times were good. More often than not he was alone, not making much of an effort to make friends. There were plenty of kids his age strolling the seaside much like he but he preferred to be by himself. On certain days he would buy a hot dog and soft pop and watch people as they passed by, with agendas of their own. Most people were still facing hardships and Coney Island was not drawing the normal crowds as years past. Though he was such a young age, JR worried about his future. Watching his mother wash floors and even scrub the toilets was troublesome to him. She, with beautiful dark hair and brown eyes and thin frame, should not be made into a workhorse. His mother worked extremely hard to ensure that there were clothes on his back and food in their stomachs. Satisfying one's appetite was anything but easy for Maeve. Often she would give her extra portions to her son who required more nourishment as a growing boy. Little did JR know, that an empty stomach for his mother, would come back to haunt her in the very near future.

24

It happened on a windy Monday in the late afternoon. Maeve had given JR a full dollar to spend at the pier. Never had she given him so much money at one time. Since he had received his latest report card with all top grades and excellent remarks, Maeve was again so proud of him. She told him not to stay out too late and to save some room for dinner. No cotton candy and taffy until after he ate his supper, she instructed. JR bolted out the front door of the rectory and ran the short distance to the amusement park. Right from the start, JR noticed the unusually empty boardwalk. The sky was gray and overcast. Only a few people braved the current weather. Wind was whipping sand off the beach and onto the boardwalk. Many people kept their heads down as to not be hit hard by the pellets of beach sand. A whirl of chaos circled the shoreline as wind swept up toward the piers. JR was fascinated by the mini tornado of sand that had begun to take great shape. Standing along the railing of the boardwalk, not too far from him, was a man who faced the ocean. He also happened to catch JR's attention. His arms were outstretched as if he was embracing the coolness of the wind which seemed to part around him. Some of the few passerby's quickly stopped behind him. Dressed in a long trench coat with the hood pulled up, it was hard to see his face. A couple of younger men passed rude comments, telling him that he was crazy. One man with his wife actually brushed past him almost knocking the stranger off balance. A small crowd now started to form around this man. As one many chimed in together shouting words like nuts, crazy and even cuckoo and told him that he should leave the beach. The chanting was even louder than the howling wind. It looked like a riot was about to start, all because an innocent man embraced the wind off the ocean. JR moved closer as the pack of people were now numbered in the teens. The lone stranger didn't flinch. He kept staring out at the water. Five men huddled in a circle as if they were devising a plan of action against this poor innocent man. JR didn't even give it a second thought or consider his own safety. He simply stood behind this man waving his arms back and forth, shouting "Show's over, nothing worth getting all fussed at. Move along people. Go home to your families and leave well enough alone." One guy who looked like he could have entered several weight lifting competitions turned toward JR and barked, "Listen runt, go home to your momma and leave the rest to us. What or why defend this apparently crazy guy paying us no attention but looking toward a sandstorm brewing." JR knew if he said the wrong thing, he would definitely cross the fine line as to what he was sure would come with some sort of whooping. JR decided it was worth the risk rather than have this poor man, who did no harm, be beaten upon by this now agitated group. Not really understanding why, he was willing to defend this complete stranger. The muscleman inched closer to JR and raised his hands as if to pick him up and toss him to the side, when suddenly a swift wind swiveled around them all. The tunnel of sand down at the shore gained velocity and was rising in its force. Instantly it veered in their direction. The crowd who only moments ago looked menacing, now scrambled away like frightened gazelles in the presence of a lion. The stranger without glancing JR's way, turned and fled. JR stood there mesmerized by the sudden viciousness of Mother Nature. No more than a minute or so had past. However once he realized that he was in the direct path of the funnel of sand, JR decided it would be wiser to take cover in a nearby alcove between the various games of chance. The high winds accompanying the sandstorm looked threatening. Even the game operators started to close their stands. Hearing metal gate after gate being pulled down over the various stands, JR squeezed in between the Clown water balloons and the penny on a plate toss. As he wedged in, JR saw someone or something sitting on a wooden milk crate with his head held in his hands.

Startled he stepped back, "Oh, excuse me. I didn't see you sitting there." Under a hooded coat, the hidden face replied, "No need to be scared son. I mean you no harm."

Sensing that his man had been weeping and looking more familiar as the darkness between the tents adjusted to his eyes, JR instantly recognized the stranger. Still not alarmed by his appearance, JR reached out, "Why are you crying. Nobody hurt you. I mean I know they said some mean stuff and all, but they didn't do what I think they wanted. I wouldn't have let them." The stranger looked up and staring at the young boy answered, "I know son. You among all those people came to my defense not even knowing who I was. Others much older and who should be wiser were willing to punish me for something so innocent such as enjoying what was created by all the laws of heaven. But you and only you were there for ME. The others, like in the past, were so fast to pass judgment." JR listened. Really listened, as this young man of no more than his mid-thirties spoke words of heaven and laws. He couldn't take his own eyes off the stranger with the beautiful piercing blue eyes. The stranger now stood and took a step closer as the wind swept his curly shoulder length brown hair. With a pointed nose of what looked to JR as a Roman soldier's, the stranger continued, "You see, that is what makes people different. You are meant for great things young man. Never lose focus. Never doubt your existence for one day, you shall be rewarded in my kingdom." Realizing that the stranger had just implied his kingdom, JR inquired, "Your kingdom. I'm only a ten-year-old boy with a dollar in my pocket. What could I possibly offer any kingdom yet alone yours." Confused by what he was hearing he continued, "You see I really don't have anything but this simple dollar. And if you need it for food, then you can have it too if you want." JR reached into his pocket and pulled out the crumpled up bill and reached out to place it in the stranger's hand. The stranger laughed in a tone that JR thought sounded like harps, the type you often heard in church at Christmas Mass. The man with the scraggly hair and blue eyes put his hand over JR's, folding JR's fingers over the money, "You of such innocence. There should be millions more of you to stop all that is designed and destined to happen in this world. Grow up and do big things for not only yourself, but for all of mankind. Keep the spirit and the fire in your heart. Don't let it ever burn you out. I will walk alongside you every chance I get, however it is up to you to walk openly with me." JR stood still, like he was frozen in time. He tried to piece together all that was said in their short conversation, but the puzzle was too big to absorb. All he could get out of his mouth was, "Who, just who exactly are you?" Without answering, the stranger edged by him and stepped out from between the tents. What was just howling, life threatening wind had ceased and now blue skies shone overhead. As fast as the storm had crept up, it vanished just as fast. The figure of the man turned to face JR and with the bright sunshine reflected behind him, he appeared to look like an angel sent from above. What the man last said would remain with JR forever. Walking backwards into the bright lights of the sun's beam, the lean man whispered, "Seamus was most certainly right, when he said what a truly special boy you were. What a special boy indeed."

25

JR grew and grew and his mother continued to adore her only son. As a teenager he looked every bit Irish as imaginable. His full head of red hair and freckles along with blue eyes and lean body, had Maeve proud of their heritage. He barely stayed after school and wasn't interested in sports. JR preferred to stay around the rectory and the few friends he did have, were only when he attended classes at school. Much of his free time was spent at Coney Island by himself. Years had passed and when JR was in his final year of high school, with only months away from graduation, a sudden illness fell upon his mother. Maeve had been having stomach pains for the past year or so and attributed it to a sparse food supply and her lack of appetite recently. For the last couple of months, many foods didn't appeal to her and at certain times the smell alone brought upon nausea. It wasn't until the constant vomiting started, that Father Bill became alarmed. Maeve was unable to keep even the tiniest amount of food down. With not enough extra weight on her petite frame, her body looked weak and frail. Father Bill took her into the city to St. Vincent's Hospital on West 12th Street in Greenwich Village. Father Bill knew a doctor there, who, before moving into Manhattan permanently, was a regular parishioner at Our Lady of Solace. After many tests and with a complete blood analysis given, the look on Doctor Graham's face was none too positive and not very promising. Maeve Ohara-Reilly had stomach cancer so far along that any treatment would not be beneficial in stopping the spread of the disease. Without any advanced medical technology, her prognosis was slim. Years of a poor diet and daily exposure to certain dusts, molds and even fumes from years of cleaning, may have caused her condition. Even the inflammation to the stomach lining attributed to the disease. Begging the doctor to be truthful about how long she would have before the cancer would claim her life, she was given six months at most. And with JR completing high school a day before his eighteenth birthday, Maeve prayed she could hang on for this special event.

26

The hardest thing Maeve ever had to do was tell the only person in the world she truly loved, that she was dying. Too weak to do any more chores around the rectory, she spent most of her time in bed. Maeve was a devout Catholic woman with a strong faith in God. She knew that she would embrace death, as much as she had embraced her short life. Her Savior waited for her in heaven, as did Seamus, the man she had always loved from the moment their eyes locked on one another. She looked forward to spending the rest of eternity with her husband. The one man other than JR that had her heart completely. So as JR entered her room, for her to break the news about her condition, something told her that her son already knew that his mother was very near death.

27

Having taken the news better than she had expected that JR would, she approached the final days before his graduation which was fast approaching. Coughing up blood, vomiting constantly, and with her stomach distended from the cancer, Maeve held on. JR rushed home right after school as he had so often over the years. He never left his mother's bedside. He would insist that the nun assigned to care for her by Father Bill in her last days, leave, so he could care for her. Maeve would smile just at the touch of his hand. Knowing her son was there kept her spirits up and encouraged her to hold on.

28

Graduation day had come and JR received top honors among his classmates. Maeve was there in the audience not missing a word, as her son spoke about what high school meant and the future for himself and his peers. Father Bill and two nuns assisted in dressing her in her Sunday best and getting her to the ceremony on time. Now thinner than ever and with difficulty breathing, Maeve sat up straighter then she had in weeks and listened to every single word her son had spoken. Upon receiving his diploma, Maeve managed to muster up enough strength to clap the loudest for her JR. As the biggest event she would ever witness came to a close, Maeve waited for her son to join them. After insisting that JR celebrate with his classmates, and because she was exhausted from the outing, she needed to go home. Seeing how his mother did everything she could to make his special day, JR made his rounds among his peers congratulating them. The biggest celebration was yet to come for JR, as he wanted nothing more than to spend the time with his mother.

29

JR was beyond delight to just be able to spend time with his mother. Together they sat in the bedroom, they had shared all these years since the passing of his father. As JR grew taller, Father Bill had added a cot in the room for him, since sharing the small bed with his mother was no longer possible. Tonight he sat on the edge and gently patted her forehead with a washcloth. Maeve, too weak to speak, knew that she had to say something to comfort her son, "You . . . have always been . . . my life. Never a day gone by . . . . that . . . . I . . . wasn't proud of . . . . you. You have always made me . . . . honored to be your . . . . mother. If I could do it . . . . all . . . . over, I wouldn't . . . . change a thing."

JR couldn't imagine life without this special woman. From cut knees, endless colds and to the many nightmares where she would stay up with him, Maeve wasn't just his mother, she was his mom. A mom like no other. Holding back the tears no longer, JR began to cry. Then he began to weep. Using his free hand, he wiped away the stream of tears that were falling down his cheeks, "Oh, momma. I love you so much. Never in my life could I love anyone the way I love you. You are my world! You always have been and always will be. Thank you mom, for everything you did for us. For me. Not a day has gone by that I wasn't grateful." Sensing the pain she was in and from the feel of her hand in his, JR knew she was slipping away. Now openly weeping he barely could get the words out, "It's ok momma. Close your eyes and go to sleep. Please don't suffer anymore. Papa is waiting for you. Papa has his arms wide open ready to hug you with all his might. Rest now and try to sleep." JR laid his head lightly down on her chest. Maeve knew the time had come and that her heavenly father was calling. With her last breath she leaned her mouth close to her son's ear and with her final dying words said, "I . . . . will . . . . love . . . . you . . . . forever . . . my . . . . son." And just like that Maeve was gone. She had kept her promise to see her son graduate high school. Maeve even made it to his eighteenth birthday, with her passing just a short fifteen minutes after midnight.

30

JR was shattered. Both his parents were gone and now he was all alone to face the world.

Father Bill made all the arrangements for his mother. At the wake, so many people came that the room was filled to capacity. People from near and far came to pay their respects to a woman who lived such a short life like her husband. Just short of her fortieth birthday, Maeve looked so beautiful in her casket. The undertaker took great measures to make her face look how it did before her illness. JR was very pleased to see the old image of his mother. The whole experience was a complete blur to poor JR. So many people had attended that he was barely able to greet them anymore. When the day had come to lower his mother to her final resting place alongside his father, JR was delusional with exhaustion. The weather was calling for rain and the skies looked ready to release a downpour at any moment. Holding an umbrella in one hand, he moved closer to the coffin. Teary eyed, he listened to Father Bill say the final prayers. Then suddenly, something off in the distance, behind a large headstone caught his eye. Wiping his eyes with his hands to make sure he wasn't seeing things, the stranger from so many years ago at the boardwalk appeared. Still in the long hooded trench coat and with the same brown wavy hair, he hadn't aged a bit. Even from afar, his piercing blue eyes shone. The stranger who now knew he had JR's attention, proceeded to walk toward the large gathering of mourners. He raised his hands high above his head and all at once the clouds parted and the sun shone brightly down upon the crowd. Everyone including Father Bill looked up to the sky in wonder and amazement. JR, however, didn't. He looked straight ahead as the stranger than lowered his arms and slid back behind the tombstone. With the sun now beating down on the whole group, JR smiled from cheek to cheek, knowing fully well, that his mother had now joined his father.

31

Father Bill, who was now nearing retirement, had just turned sixty-three. The diocese had been exceptionally kind to allow him to stay at Our Lady of Solace. With the country now back on an uphill economic climb, employment was on the rise again. World War II had ended just two years prior with the loss of many Jews in Germany. A madman named Adolf Hitler, so delusional as to think he could create a superior race, sent millions of innocent people to their deaths. The United States joined forces with other countries to help free many remaining Jews left in concentration camps to die as defeat seemed inevitable.

America was back on its feet and once again noted as the most powerful country in the world. Father Bill knew that soon he would retire from his beloved parish and live among the other retired priests at a different rectory. His time at Our Lady of Solace was very limited. Maybe he would be granted another two years at most. With the absence of JR's parent, Father Bill assumed the role as his guardian. Actually more as a surrogate parent. Father Bill felt that JR was more of a son to him since the little boy came to live at the rectory, when he was no more than two. Father Bill wanted to ensure that with the proper education, JR could and would succeed in this world. Since JR loved numbers, one night he sat down with JR and mentioned the idea of becoming an accountant. JR was very enthusiastic to continue his studying in that field. After several phone calls and calling in many favors of his fellow priests, JR was enrolled in college by summers end. JR would major in the principle of accounting finance program at Saint Francis College in Brooklyn Heights. The college had been founded in 1859 and was a staple among catholic parishioners. The dean of admissions had been a personal friend of Father Bill's since they had been in the Seminary at the same time studying for the priesthood. The issue of tuition was discussed at length among the old friends and an arrangement had been made for JR to attend. Father Bill was pleased that he was able to help this young man pursue a dream, which could now be fulfilled. JR would make a name for himself in the corporate world. Of that, Father Bill was certain. The only other certainty was, that Father Bill wouldn't live to see it.

32

The year was 1948 and JR had just finished his sophomore year. As he attended his junior year at Saint Francis College, life was looking better than it had for JR in the past. Each semester he had made the Dean's list and was a fine example among the other students. For extra cash, JR tutored others in math and accounting. Most of his free time consisted of teaching such subjects. With Christmas break just days away, JR looked forward to spending the quiet holidays with Father Bill, who now resided on Long Island in a retirement home in the Diocese of Rockville Centre. Father Bill would be picking him up on Friday for the extended two-week vacation. Father Bill had one sister who lived in Bellmore and she always opened her home to JR for the holidays. Recently widowed, with no children of her own, she welcomed young JR and her brother to spend the time with her, on this most blessed holiday season.

With the weather forecast calling for more than a foot of snow for Friday, JR worried that his plans may be cancelled and he would have to stay in the dorms by himself, while all the others went home. After receiving the phone call on Friday morning from Father Bill, he was reassured that no storm, large or small, would keep the good Father from picking him up. Told to have his bags packed and ready to go, Father Bill was leaving in the very early am on Friday to beat the approaching storm. Unfortunately the storm beat him before the full impact of the winter covering even arrived.

33

It wouldn't be until late Friday as the night made way for Saturday, that JR would be paid a visit by Dean McNally. As JR sat with worry and concern about why it was taking Father Bill so long to arrive, the snow had now accumulated to over thirteen inches. Transportation was nearly impossible. JR knew there would be no way Father Bill could make the drive in this snowstorm. Promised that he would leave at the dawn's early light, JR's stomach was so knotted that he felt ill. Something was not right.

As he lay down on his dorm bed, the knock that he waited and prayed for it to be Father Bill finally came. Knowing all along it wouldn't be the man he prayed for, his prayers were not answered. Dean McNally, entered the room, and sat in the chair opposite his bed as JR rose to sit up. The dean looked ashen faced himself. He had known Father Bill for many many years and just by his expression alone, JR knew that once again tragedy had struck. Reports by drivers of the other vehicles at the scene stated that Father Bill lost complete control of his car, on a patch of ice. The Belt Parkway, near Coney Island was the location. Trying to steer into the skid, at a speed a bit too fast, the car hit the guardrail and flipped. Several inches of snow had covered the ice from the previous night's freezing temperatures. Father Bill, who wasn't wearing a seatbelt, was thrown from the car. Paramedics on the crash site determined that he had died upon impact with the guardrail. He suffered a broken neck, and was already dead before the aftermath of the accident and being thrown from the vehicle. Somewhat comforted that it was a quick death for the man, who he came to love as much as his parents, JR again, was devastated. Never did he again in his life want to open up his heart and love someone unconditionally. The hurt was too painful. For reasons he could never fully understand, JR felt as if some force was testing him. Both his parents and now Father Bill were truly spiritual people who believed in a faith and a God so powerful. JR questioned how any God could let this happen to such wonderful and special people. In his twenty years of life, JR suffered more losses than most people his age. Emotionally he was finished with letting people into his heart and made a promise to not allow his love to blind him. Death seemed to follow his every step. It was blackness so open as to shatter his soul and the ones around him. JR would watch his every step and keep his distance from letting himself become attached. And if that didn't work, then JR was certain, he would live a lifetime of death and despair. After all, twenty years was a fraction of time in a person's existence. For all the loss he experienced, if he lived a full life, JR feared just how many people he would love, would die.

34

Father Bill's ceremony was like nothing JR would have ever imagined. Taking place between the holiest of weeks after the birth of Jesus, made it somewhat easier for JR. A lifetime of devotion was given by Father Bill to his maker. Coincidentally, he left this world just two days prior to the arrival of baby Jesus that Christmas day. People from every walk of life attended all the services. Priests, pastors, and monsignors from afar turned out to bid a fond farewell to a dear man. A lifetime of sacrifice to the faith he so deeply cherished, Father Bill had left his legacy. Eulogy after eulogy praised a man who helped many over his lifetime. At times, there was not a dry eye in the church. After the burial, at the same cemetery as his parents, Father Bill's sister approached JR. She, too, took his passing extremely hard. Upon saying their final goodbyes, she left JR with an open invitation to her home. JR was welcome to stay there once he graduated college. Her door would always be open to this fine young man who endured so much loss. JR, however, knew that door would never be entered by him. For to enter her house, Father Bill's sister like all the others he ever loved, would succumb to an uncertain death before her time.

Never to cross that threshold, in fear of harm to someone he also cared about, JR graciously accepted the offer, with no intention of ever taking her up on it.

35

So there you have it my friends. The first chapter in Jack Rogan Reilly's life. Some of you will say that my early formative years were very tragic. Others will chalk it up to life's experiences and the misfortunes people suffer. I, for one, had just started to learn what my exact purpose in life was. Nothing. That's right, you read it here first. Absolutely nothing or so I thought. Here I was a twenty-year old at the brink of a new decade. I had finished school and earned my degree at Saint Francis College. With highly polished recommendation letters from Dean McNally, I was offered three different job offers to choose, at very successful established accounting firms in mid-town Manhattan. I interviewed with all three and chose the largest firm, in hopes of just blending in with the other accountants You see, at this stage of my life, all I ever wanted to do was to blend in and live my life in shadows and not be noticed. For quite some time that is exactly what I did until I was about to hit a milestone birthday, when my life would change forever.

36

Before that takes place, there are so many world events of more importance. Some have made their mark in the history books and others came and went. Sort of like a fad. I'll explain more in detail in a bit. Leaving behind my few college friends, who drifted off to start careers of their own, I was once again left alone. Choosing different career paths in life, meant heading in opposite directions, never to reconnect. First, I started working for Roger Wilson of Wilson Textiles on 47th Street between 8th & 9th Avenues in New York City. Immediately landing the job, I no longer wanted to commute from Brooklyn into the city. Too many commuters crammed in a subway reminded me of when you open a can of sardines and they are all neatly stacked next to one another. Although I don't eat sardines, I've seen the can in the grocery store and just assumed that is the layout. So after asking around the office to the employees I might have considered friends, I was told that Greenwich Village would be the best location. With an uptown bus that ran straight up to Central Park, it became obvious that this would suit me well. I signed a two-year lease with an elderly man in one of his brownstones. Mr. Schmidt, wrinkled well beyond his seventy-five years, rented the third floor studio apartment to me. He had renovated the old attic into a small living arrangement for added income. This small living arrangement consisted of one room. I was able to fit a bed along with a dresser and a tiny nightstand against the wall as you entered the room. My bathtub located in the kitchen served as both a bath and table. There was a small piece of plywood to cover the tub's opening and to miraculously transform it into a fully operational eating area. After all, I was the only one to sit there. The refrigerator, stove, and sink stood next to one another on the far wall opposite my bed. For most, my living arrangements would make them shutter with bouts of claustrophobia, but it was just the right space for me. I would eventually stay there in this one tiny room, for most of my life. Mr. Schmidt would pass on and leave it to his two daughters, in turn who would eventually sell the building to a real estate mogul. Thankfully, it was rent stabilized and protected by New York Housing. The way my life and luck downward spiraled, one would have bet I would have been tossed into the street reminiscent of what had happened a long time ago, the story which my dearest mother had shared with me. For the time being I was spared the humiliation.

37

Time moved on and soon the decade of the 1950's was in full swing. The Korean War began in 1950, but since I was considered an orphan, I wasn't drafted. My last name needed to be carried on. Trying to serve the country I so admired, I went to enlist and because of my flat feet, was denied enrollment in any branch of the military service. It just wasn't in the cards for me. Bigger things lie ahead. Music was now the era of rock and roll and the King of them all was born from it. Elvis Presley took or should I say shook the nation by storm. A tough looking movie star, actor James Dean, died in a car accident. Reports all stated his young life was cut too short with a promising film career ahead of him. The polio vaccine was created, and a magic kingdom for young children called Disneyland opened. A crazy fad of a circular plastic ring that everyone twirled around their hips was known as the Hula Hoop. A place to grab a burger, with a funny looking red-headed clown as its mascot, named McDonalds became popular. Television shows hit the airwaves. I Love Lucy was an instant hit, in which a red head, her Cuban husband and her crazy antics entertained audiences everywhere. The Howdy Doody Show was one of the first and easily the most popular children's television show in the 1950s. Howdy, himself, was a red-headed, freckled faced puppet. Then there was Jack Rogan Reilly, also a red-headed freckled face young man. With the sudden explosion of popular red heads, I was not as fortunate, since my new nickname at work was Doody. All the exposure to the color red didn't benefit me. It actually turned the color of my blood a deeper red than I thought possible.

You see, red had fast become my least favorite color.

38

The decadent fifties has progressed, but I remained the same. According to some, my parents and Father Bill, I did not achieve any substantial status. Any high hopes of me achieving or even making a name for myself, wasn't happening any time soon. I wasn't wealthy, nor did I acquire fame and fortune in patenting an invention. I lived a simple life. A hum drum one at that. Every morning at the crack of dawn I would wake and after a meager breakfast of a boiled egg and two pieces of toast, along with a glass of orange juice, I prepared a ham and cheese sandwich with an apple for lunch. Occasionally, if there was a sale I might treat myself to some cookies as a snack. People may classify me as cheap but I would say I was more along the lines of frugal. I ate relatively the same food every day Monday through Friday. Every night I would bathe and lay out my business suit for the next day at the office. I shopped on

Saturdays and laundered my clothes on that day as well. Sunday, I attended early mass at Saint Patrick's Cathedral and would splurge for breakfast at a mid-town diner. After a nice stroll through the city streets, I would retire for the evening to read the New York Times in its entirety. My life had become very predictable. My routine never deviated. I would catch the same bus to my job as an accountant for a textiles company who occupied the first three floors in a twelve floor building. There was a warehouse next store where we manufactured our own products. The company employed two hundred and fifty people, none of whom I had established any real friendships with. I arrived at eight am each morning, did my job alongside two dozen fellow accountants, and left promptly at five pm. I ate my lunch in the company cafeteria on the third floor by myself. On occasion, I would sit with a few of the other men in my department to try to fit in. I wasn't too fond of most of them, since they all had families of their own and I didn't. Of course that was my choice to remain single. Each of them bragged how beautiful their wives were or how their kids were the smartest. They even spoke how well-trained their dog was. Too much conversation about themselves and themselves only, didn't help make me feel any better. Often I would pass on the invitation to join them and resort to the crossword puzzles in the newspaper. Most of them knew I preferred to be alone and didn't press the subject for company at lunch. That suited me just fine. Until the day that a not-so-nice gentleman by the name of Michael Sullivan was hired.

39

As luck would have it, Mike was also an accountant and was seated at the desk right next to mine. The only common denominators we shared, were that we were both Irish and about the same age. There were no other comparisons to be made. We were as similar as oil was to water. Where I was a real life Howdy Doody, Mike was a jet black haired, green-eyed darker complexion individual. I stood at six feet and he at a more muscular five foot ten. Mike assumed since we were both two of the only eligible bachelors at the company, we should as he put it, pal out. For weeks on end, he would try to get me to go to some of the local bars for a beer after work. Not liking the taste of any alcoholic beverages, I always refused. Then after an unfortunate incident, my life concerning my employment, would become my latest hell. Mike was leaning over my desk and trying to intimidate me into hanging with him, "What's the matter red? You too good to tag along with the likes of me? For the last few months, I keep asking and you never want to come. I thought maybe, since you look like you may need an outlet, I'd help a co-worker out. I'll even let you have the first pick of the ladies."

Annoyed as I was at how conceited and self-centered this guy was, I tried not to irk him, "I appreciate the constant offers, really I do. It's just that I . . . ."

"You, what red? Don't like women."

"No, not at all. Please don't put words in my mouth. I just prefer not to . . . ."

Past the point of being friendly now, Mike had heard enough excuses regarding the past few offers. "What. Wait. So what I'm hearing and correct me if I'm wrong. You like women? Right?"

I knew he expected some sort of reply so I just shook my head yes.

"Okay, so we're both clear that you do like women. Then it must be something else."

Raising one hand off my desk, he scratched his chin, "Could it be me then? I would hope not. But I would have to assume that if you like women. And you just nodded yes. Then what else could it be. After all, being you live a pathetic existence . . . ."

Steaming now and not able to hold back after that last statement, I raised my voice, "Pathetic existence Mike. Really. Is that how you feel about me? Then why bug me to go out with you, all the time."

Mike stood straight up and noticed that all the other men in the office now were locked into the heated conversation. Not wanting to look like he had just been spoken to in a loud tone, and embarrassed by a red-headed guy that he just wanted to befriend, he blasted right back, "Why? Do you really want to know why. I'll tell you why. YOU, are such a mess. I mean look at you! What a poor excuse for an Irishman. A face full of freckles and that lanky body of yours. I guess if they needed an extra to play the scarecrow in The Wizard of Oz, look no further."

A couple of the men chuckled at the last comment Mike made.

Jack didn't know what to do or where to turn, as he sat in his chair letting this Adonis tear him to shreds. Face blushing so red that he felt his cheeks wanting to explode, he pushed back his chair to get up and leave the area. Mike saw Jack's face turning beet red and knew he had won. Not wanting him to escape this tirade before the final blow and punch to the gut Mike laughed, "Jeez, and to think I could have been your friend. What the heck was I thinking? You probably like to sit home and watch television like the sad little creature you are. Too bad you couldn't catch that kiddie show in the mornings that my nephews enjoy. What's that show called?" Again he scratched his chin, knowing all eyes were on him and pretended to remember, "The Howdy Doody Show. That's who you are! Right guys?" He looked over at his co-workers, who now had joined in on the laughter. "It's Howdy Doody time everyday right here for us too!"

40

And there you have it. My new nickname in my office was born. At least once a morning one of the guys would pass a snide remark. I would hear someone say Howdy to one of the other men who walked into our work area. Shortly after, another would yell it's our Doody to do a good job today. Several would look at me and say, "Isn't that right, it sits here with us. We all have our Doody." Hilarious outburst would come from everyone, but mostly from Mike who was the loudest. He would push back his chair and pat his knees as he laughed hysterically. I, on the other hand, would try to ignore them. But they would all know differently, since my face would turn the color I so hated.

41

I had just celebrated my tenth anniversary, at a company, I no longer enjoyed working for. But the fact of the matter was, I didn't like change either. I would stick it out regardless. I tolerated the other men and didn't even flinch at the name Doody anymore. I had a scheduled meeting with Mr. Wilson at ten am. Truthfully, I wasn't afraid it had anything to do with my work performance, since I was the best of the group when it came to finances. He did, however, allow the other men to basically torture me. He must have heard the continuous laughter on certain mornings, since his office was within earshot of where we all sat. Perhaps it had become a distraction to his staff and to resolve the issue, he would terminate the problem from where it stemmed. That morning I did a lot of praying before I walked into his office. Roger Wilson, a self-made man, was in his fifties. He lived and breathed his fortune. At a fraction under six feet, he had brown eyes and buzzed cut brown hair. Along with his tan complexion, he looked more suited for an outdoors man, instead of the workaholic he was.

"Please, have a seat JR."

Not many had called me JR anymore, so I was surprised to hear that. I took a seat across from him.

"Relax JR. First I would like to thank you for the past ten years of loyalty to me and my company. Its good men like you that continue to make my business the success it is."

Shaking my head for a brief second to make sure I was hearing correctly I nervously answered, "Thank you Sir. Thank you for noticing. I mean I really appreciate that." Not having had many conversations with this man I knew my words were shaky.

Roger Wilson liked Jack Reilly. Out of all his accountants he was the most brilliant.

Without making JR more uncomfortable, he stood up and walked over to his window.

Looking out at the hustle and bustle of the passersbys, he spoke more softly, "Point is JR. I devoted most of my life to building what I like to call MY mini-empire. With just Gladys and myself, our life has been pretty good. I make the money and she spends it; mostly at the country club. I would like to be able to join her at some of what she likes to call outlandish luncheons. Of course I would come back to the office. But in my absence I need someone to supervise the department, a take-charge individual."

Hearing but not hearing where I thought this conversation was going I questioned my boss, "So what you are looking for is someone to run things for you? Supervise the finance department? Is that correct Sir?"

"Absolutely JR. Just these bunch of buffoons. Dolores, the office manager, can handle the other departments as she has in the past. Irene, my secretary, will also be available if things should get out of hand."

"Why would things get out of hand Sir?"

Turning away from the glass, Roger Wilson now faced JR, "Listen JR. You are the man I want to lead the team. You have the most smarts. I know you don't think so. You JR, are very intelligent and have been very good to me. Now don't get offended or insulted by what I say next. I just started hearing the other men and what they say around the office about you. Especially the likes of Mike. Don't let them get to you. With this promotion, you call all the shots. No one has the right to speak to any employee of mine in a negative way. Dolores and Irene have mentioned this to me on several occasions but I've been too absorbed in the business to take notice. Even though my door to my office is open, I seem to block the noise out. Recently I heard a comment myself and informed the person to spread the word that it stops now. Have you noticed a change?"

I couldn't absorb all that was being said to me. Promotion, the women telling him about my ridiculing, too much sinking in at once. And after all, the others including Mike had let up on me the last couple of days.

"JR, you did hear me. Has there been a change around the office the last day or two?"

Finally getting a grasp of all he had said and what he was asking, I said, "Yes, Sir. I have noticed the change. Thank you Sir. Thank you."

"You are very welcome JR. Consider this a new beginning to you. With the end of hopefully all this rock and roll stuff, let's hope the next decade is better. So is that a yes to your new title as my Finance Manager as well? If so, we'll get that little storage room that hasn't been used in years cleaned up and make it your own office. What'da ya say to that?"

Bewildered, appreciative, and oh so grateful, I again answered with more confidence this time, since my nerves had now calmed down but my adrenaline was all pumped up, "I gladly accept your offer and I know I will make more of an impact for you and an influence all around. You have my promise on that." A promise I had every intention of keeping.

42

For me, life had gotten somewhat better. After all I was now the immediate supervisor to the guys who had ridiculed me every chance they had. No longer did they make fun of me, but there were times that Doody or Howdy was uttered under bated breaths. Mike, who was having the most difficulty having to report directly to me, was most guilty of this behavior. I wasn't a difficult boss, but I did put more pressure and imposed deadlines on the group as a payback for all the abuse I suffered. Over time, as a department we worked smoothly. As I said previously, the majority of the men in my department were family men with mortgages and mouths to feed. No one wanted to walk the streets in hopes of finding their next means of support. Each day I would arrive at work, continue to do what I always did, and watch as life just flew by.

43

Psycho scared movie goers. A British group with a bug's name, The Beatles, had swept almost every young American girl off their feet. A blonde bombshell, Marilyn Monroe, was found dead of a drug overdose. Her career as a movie actress was flourishing at the time. Liked to the Kennedy brothers, active politicians in our country, was assumed to play a role in her untimely death at an early age. Then came all the assassinations. John F. Kennedy, who eventually became our president, was shot first. Malcolm X, a courageous advocate for the rights of African Americans, was next. Then Martin Luther King Jr., a voice for the equality of all, was killed. Robert F. Kennedy, JFK's brother, was the last to have his life cut short. The nation was rocked by all this tragedy. It seemed that every year or so another assassination occurred that shocked the country and sent Americans into panic. Then the United States did what most Americans thought impossible. An Astronaut, Neil Armstrong, became the first man to walk on the moon. A phrase was coined, 'One small step for man; one giant step for mankind' gave hope again to all that was lost. At the close of the 1960's, a rock and roll concert, held in Woodstock paved the way for the 1970's and the younger generation who would come to be known as flower children and hippies.

44

Now as a man in my early forties, I was still living a boring life. Society had taken a complete turn as many teenagers and young adults now protested war. Rallies and demonstrations had crowds of great proportions and riots would ensue. Local law enforcement would need to be present at these assemblies to control the crowds. Screams and shouts of 'Peace not war!' could be heard over the various speakers in favor of military combat. The change in the new generation of young people amazed me. Back in my younger days, lines of young men were enlisting for the chance to keep the country safe. Today's young men were dodging the draft by leaving the United States to avoid serving the land of the free. The country faced one of the biggest scandals involving President Nixon. The affair began with the arrest of five men for breaking and entering into the Democratic National Committee headquarters at the Watergate complex on June 17, 1972. The FBI connected the payments to the burglars to a slush fund used by the 1972 Committee to Re-elect the President. As evidence mounted against the president's staff, which included former staff members testifying against them in an investigation conducted by the Senate Watergate Committee, it was revealed that President Nixon had a tape recording system in his offices and that he had recorded many conversations. Recordings from these tapes implicated the president, revealing that he had attempted to cover up the break-in. After a series of court battles, the U.S. Supreme Court ruled that the president had to hand over the tapes; he ultimately complied. With a shaky government, the American people again were left uncertain. Overseas at the Olympic Games in Munich, our first terrorist attack occurred. Many more of greater impact were to follow. And I, Jack Rogan Reilly, like a programmed robot faced each day like the last. Nothing really caught me off guard or by total surprise. America had indeed come a long way. Some say for the better, others for the worse. I didn't have an opinion either way. I now took showers instead of baths. Never did or would have the desire to drive, so a license wasn't ever acquired. Radio shows led to television programs. Black and white televisions were replaced by color. A miniseries aptly titled 'Roots' had every television in our country tuned in at some part. Martin Luther King Jr., would be proud. I, on the other hand, was fast approaching half a century of life the following year. Dateless, loveless and all alone, I watched time tick by. Little did I know that a chance at love might be blossoming, or so I thought.

45

Christmas 1977 led to the start of another year. I, for one, never understood how some people cried at the New Year. Was it for past dearly departed family members that no longer walked the earth, or the excitement of the unknown. It was just another year for me and a year closer to the day, I could put all this work behind me and ride off into retirement. A lifetime of aging with no real purpose. Something most would look forward to. I was still years away for now. My job still was the only focus of my life. Things at the office were basically the same, until an opening for a senior accountant position became available. Steve Malone, the office optimist, had reached sixty- two and was ready to pack it in. He and his wife had talked for years about retiring to sunny Florida. Since Steve had enjoyed fly-fishing, year round warm temperatures would allow just that. Listing the house on the real estate market, Steve sold his house sooner than expected. After giving his two-week notice, Steve said his goodbyes and left New York for golden aged retirement. He was one of the few I would truly miss. This left an immediate opening within our department. Concerning any accounting issue, Mr. Wilson had left the hiring process up to me as well. An ad was placed in the New York Times and applicants were instructed to send their resumes to my attention. A week later a dozen or so had been left on my desk. I picked up a bunch. With women now just as active in the work force, there were a few resumes from females. I briefly scanned them. One in particular caught my eye. With a very extensive work background, it looked like a perfect fit to fill Steve's position. In fact, it was exactly what I was looking for. I called the phone number listed on her resume and left a message to set up an interview. The very next day Victoria Hillbrandt called. Eager to meet this candidate who, from the brief phone call sounded sensuous, I couldn't wait for the day to be over. Tomorrow couldn't come fast enough. Only afterward, I would have wished it had never come at all.

46

That evening I had great difficulty falling asleep. The anticipation to meet this soft spoken woman was overwhelming. Twice in the middle of the night, I suddenly woke up.

Never before had I been so restless, as to wake up before the early morning hours. Finally realizing that I would not be counting anymore sheep, I rose from bed. Normally I would take a shower the night before as I had last evening. However, with all the tossing and turning, I figured another hot shower might calm my nerves. Looking at my reflection in the mirror, I tried to ask myself what it was from a woman's voice that could get me this worked up. Never before had I experienced feelings like this. My heart raced, my palms felt clammy, in anticipation of our meeting. Convincing myself that she was an unattractive much older woman on the hefty side, had worked for the time being. I was able to finish dressing in my best suit, eat my full breakfast that left me still a bit queasy, and hurry out my front door. No need to get all worked up if the woman turned out to be an ugly duckling. So once convinced that her looks would be oh so plain, Jack Rogan Reilly, would soon find out, how totally wrong he really was.

47

Victoria Hillbrandt was a stunningly beautiful thirty-five-year-old woman. Standing an impressive five foot nine with shoulder length blonde hair and blue eyes the color of the ocean, she entered my office at precisely the time we agreed upon. Instantly I felt my knees quiver. Not only was she attractive, she was breathtaking. Every eye in the office, both those of men and women, followed her as she moved her body along so elegantly. From a distance and before she entered my office, I gasped and found it hard to catch a breath. As she stood before me, I wiped my hand on my pant leg as I also stood up to shake her hand in a formal gesture. Immediately she locked eyes with mine. I felt like I had been put into some sort of spell; a trance of which could not be broken. Taking my hand in hers, I barely managed a hello. We both sat down at the same moment. She sat across my desk. Trying to stay focused and trying to keep my composure, I began by saying, "Thank you for being punctual." Not knowing what to say next I continued, "Is it Miss or Mrs. Hillbrandt if you don't mind me asking?"

Still staring intensely into my eyes she replied, "Why the formalities? Call me Vicky. Most of my friends and colleagues call me that. Besides, to get right to the point, as you can see, I do believe that I meet all your required criteria for the ad you placed in the paper. I come highly qualified and am sure to please in any way I can. Also, I prefer you call me by my first name. Miss sounds so old fashioned. And since I never found the right man to settle down with, so, yes, it is miss but it just seems so formal." Victoria now crossed her legs and showed enough skin to arouse even a blind man.

I couldn't believe what I was hearing. Or seeing, which now had my full attention above and below the waist. She was talking to me like we had known each other for months rather than a brief moment. I had many business encounters during my career and this woman was a first in coming to an interview so relaxed and forward. Usually the tables are turned the other way around and she should be the one all jittery and nervous. Still shaken and with perspiration now dotting my forehead, I was hoping it wasn't noticeable. I also smelled a fragrance of perfume that brought tears to my eyes. The aroma was astonishing. The smallest whiff of it and she had me at hello. Captivated by her beauty, I asked "Of course Vicky and you may call me JR. JR is for Jack Reilly, really Jack Rogan Reilly as written on my birth certificate. Some call me Jack but I prefer JR, . . ." I stopped myself mid-sentence. I couldn't believe what was coming out of my mouth. I was babbling and couldn't be stopped. Afraid to stand for fear she would notice my erection, I dared not move from my seat. I needed to gain control of the situation, if I were to gain any respect from this potential candidate for the open position. Although at that moment, I knew I wouldn't be interviewing another person, male or female. Vicky had the position the minute I laid eyes on her.

48

The two weeks preceding her start date felt like an eternity to me. I couldn't wait for each day to end, so that I could go home, sleep, so that the next day would arrive. I repeated this process for the two weeks until the big day. While waiting for Vicky to start with us, I restructured the department including desk placements. Mike Sullivan, who unfortunately still worked for us, was placed the farthest back in the room. I rearranged everyone so that the desk directly in front of my office was empty.

I longed for Vicky to be as close to me as possible, without raising a red flag to the rest of my staff. Even if they did question why, I could care less as long as this mesmerizing woman sat closest to me. With all finally in place, the time had finally arrived. After giving her former employer the standard two-week notice, Vicky started her career at Wilson Textiles.

49

That morning, I arrived at the office earlier than usual. Dressed more for a wedding than a regular Monday at the office, I even stopped to get a shoe shine. I wanted to look sharp. Since good looks wasn't something I was born with, I had to pull out all the stops in order to enhance my appearance. A cross of Howdy Doody meets Ronald McDonald best described me. Like it or not, that is who I was. I watched the large clock situated high on the wall across the room as each minute ticked to the next. As the tick tock grew louder, I looked down on my desk at the pen holder with the little built in clock to see if another minute had passed. Afterward, I would then glance at my wristwatch too, in hopes of nine o'clock appearing on its face. When every desk in the office was filled with my group of men, the last person to enter was, indeed, Vicky. Slowly she entered the room, aware of every eye fixated on her. Her hips swayed back and forth as she proceeded to cross the room. When she finally reached my door, she knocked lightly, "Morning, JR. Seeing all these here desks are taken and this front one being vacant, I gather that's where I'll be sitting my pretty ole self down then. Is that right?"

Remembering their initial interview, and the fact that she was raised in the south before moving to New York, I enjoyed her southern accent very much. What I didn't appreciate was her directness. Seriously, it was her first day and already she was making assumptions as to where she would sit. Ironically enough though, Vicky was right. She called it, as she would be calling all the shots, before I would even be able to put a stop to it.

50

Vicky proved her knowledge of accounting the first few weeks. Having come from a totally different type of company manufacturing, her quick understanding of our accounting principles was evident. More often than not, she somehow managed to spend time next to me in my office. Her questions were always specific and valid. Unable to completely understand her ploy in managing to get me to stop my work, I always complied. I found myself showing Vicky every aspect of Wilson Textiles financial records which were strictly confidential material. She had a way of persuading me, not so much with words, rather than body language. I didn't want to let her leave my office and on numerous times I even allowed her to pull up a chair right alongside me. Vicky showed extreme interest in every bit of financial information I was willing to show. Often after business hours, she would come to my door and just start a conversation of no real importance with me. Clearly she knew she had me at her beckon call. Tossing her long golden locks from side to side in a very seductive manner, she would lean her slim body against my door. Rather than come through the door, Vicky would tap her slender finger up and down the doorjamb. Knowing that all the men in my department spoke behind my back with idle gossip about my favoritism toward Vicky, it still didn't even bother me. Normally most of our dialogue was harmless, but at times Vicky would come awfully close to crossing that fine line. As a man who ate his lunch alone in his office, she would walk in and start with some sort of sexual innuendo.

One day in particular came to mind, as she leaned over me with her low cut red dress on, exposing more of her breast than I had ever seen from a woman. Breathing softly over my ear, she whispered "Why do you eat your lunch every day all by your lonesome? Don't you ever get lonely?"

Aroused but trying to keep the conversation low key, I answered "I prefer to eat my meals alone rather than with company I do not enjoy." Realizing I may have just upset her I continued, "Not that your company would not be enjoyable. What I mean is that anytime you want to share a meal. Say even dinner, I'm available. I'm free any night you want me."

"Why ain't that just sweet. Not only are you asking me to dinner but I do believe you are flirting with me JR. Are you?"

"Am I what?"

"Certainly you remember what ya just said. Something about dinner and little ole me joining you. Isn't that just peachy of you."

For the safety of my title, position and the fact I was her immediate supervisor, I tried desperately to reel the conversation back in, "Vicky, honestly. As a co-worker, I would so enjoy making time for you outside of business hours but on a professional level, I simply shouldn't, couldn't go there."

"Oh JR, don't fret over it. I only just started working for you. Give it some time and let's see where this all ends up. After all, us Southern ladies have a certain way in charming you Yankee boys. Like I always say, after Vicky, you all come back now real soon."

And just like that, Vicky giggled, turned and left my office in a flash. I, on the other hand, was more flustered than I had ever been in my entire life. My desire for this woman was inconceivable, the lust alone unimaginable, and the truth of the matter, I stood a better chance of freezing in hell before winning her over.

51

Just a week short of my fiftieth birthday and somehow by the grace of God, I managed to keep my feelings for Vicky under control. She still came into my office each and every day but instead of flirting, we got down to business. Insisting that she help lighten my workload, I allowed it. Eventually I even entrusted her with all of my work. Most of my accounting dealt with the overall finances of the entire company. I, in turn, was given the task of making all the deposits and transfers of the capital of the organization. Having been with Mr. Wilson for more years than I cared to count, he seemed to rely on me for each and every financial transaction. As he had stated on more than one occasion in the past, he believed me to be his most loyal and devoted employee, who looked out for the best interest of the company. For that I was grateful, until the day when all that would suddenly change.

52

As you may see, while I had totally let my guard down, Vicky, along with Mike Sullivan had devised a plan of their own. Failing to see that an instant mutual attraction existed between them, I was blinded by my own carelessness for true beauty. I should have known that someone as breathtaking as Vicky, would never have an interest in the likes of me. Looking back, there were several times that I had seen both Vicky and Mike chatting, either at the copier or water cooler. I would catch them laughing and joking too, when I would get my lunch from the refrigerator. I didn't give much thought to that, since I thought she only had eyes for me. Little did I know. While laundering the company money into a joint account they opened with fake identities and a false business, they continuously forged my name on certain documents. Somehow they made it so legitimate that it couldn't be traced back to them. If and when the auditors checked up on the general ledger books, all evidence of the stealing would point to me and me alone. Thousands upon thousands of dollars had been embezzled from Wilson Textiles and deposited into a business named

H.D. Inc. Later I would find out that the H.D. was in honor of me. But I would be anything but honored when it turned out that the initials stood for Howdy Doody. Before I even had the chance to piece anything together, the floor was about to drop out from under me the very next day.

53

Arriving at my usual time, I was greeted by the building security guards. With no explanation, they both escorted me to my office where Mr. Wilson sat in my chair. Confused, I asked what was going on, although just by the look on Mr. Wilson's face, I knew something bad had happened. With a wave of his hand in dismissal, one security guard closed the door, leaving just the two of us alone. Explaining in great detail about certain funds missing and without any proof of where the money disappeared to, all fingers pointed at me. He had lost an exorbitant amount of cash. Money he had worked hard for his entire life, only to lose it by someone he had trusted. Roger Wilson, having just turned seventy, had recently announced he would be retiring. In all likelihood, among rumors that also circulated around the office, I would be promoted to Chief Financial Officer, left running his empire. Now with hard core evidence in black and white against me personally, that dream was shattered. Mr. Wilson continued to rant and rave for the next several minutes, all the while accusing me of some act I did not commit. For that matter, wasn't even aware of until that very moment. I was flabbergasted at his continued accusations. I felt my whole body begin to break out in a cold sweat. Trying to explain that I had absolutely no idea what he was implying, the conversation suddenly escalated. Mr. Wilson fired me on the spot. He told me that my services were no longer needed. In order to save his reputation and that of his company, charges would not be filed. He didn't want to involve the federal investigators or even the local authorities for that matter. Until he could pinpoint the actual crimes which were committed, I was simply instructed to pack my personal belongings of almost the past thirty years and to vacate the premises immediately. He also told me that if I ever showed my face within a two – block radius of his building, he would take matters into his own hands. And just like that, I was escorted out of the building, while my co-workers of so many years, stared at me in disbelief. Vicky stood alongside Mike smirking as I passed.

54

As I carried my briefcase in one hand and wheeled three boxes on my luggage carrier that I had purchased years ago and never used, I walked aimlessly down the street. All I kept asking myself was how this could have happened. How could I have been so stupid as to let funds be laundered by someone I couldn't place. Then all at once it hit me. Victoria Hillbrandt had set me up. All along I thought that just maybe I stood a chance of winning over her affection. Boy was I wrong. She used me and hung me out to dry. For what reason, I vowed, I would find out. I decided to return the very next morning extremely early, and wait for her to get close to the building. I knew I was taking a chance, since I could wind up endangering my well-being. Either I would be locked up by the police or Mr. Wilson might physically attack me. I had no other choice but to confront her and find out the truth. How bad could it actually be? After all, it was my fiftieth birthday tomorrow and half my life was already over. Sadly enough, at that moment, I didn't realize I might never see the other half.

55

Happy Birthday to me, as I waited three blocks away from Wilson Textiles. For early April, the weather was warmer than usual. I didn't grab a jacket as I left my apartment. I just kept going over everything in my head. Thankfully, I knew exactly where to wait. In one of our many conversations, Vicky had told me her direct path to work. Having lived on the upper west side, she would walk the twenty blocks down and then cut across from Tenth Avenue to the building. Since the West Side was less busy than the East Side of Manhattan, there were less people walking the streets to their jobs this early in the morning. Then, off in the distance I spotted her at precisely the same moment that both she and that dirty scum of a man, Mike Sullivan, spotted me. They were holding hands as lovers often do. How could I have been so stupid? She let go of his hand. Mike headed in a different direction after she placed a hand on his shoulder. I guessed she told him to head to the office so she could handle it, because she came up to me first, "Well lookie who we got here. How's unemployment suiting the likes of you?"

Not believing how I could have let this woman of such outer beauty outsmart me I replied, "I know what you did. As long as there is a God, I will do everything I can to prove my innocence."

"Know what I did. Look at you accusing ME!" her sweet soft spoken voice now took on a life of its own, "Why you silly little piece of shit. Treating Mike the way YOU did! A kind, loving, gentle, compassionate man and you made him feel inferior."

Losing control myself I shouted, "Mike Sullivan compassionate! Are you kidding me. How did he fool you? Wait, he never fooled you. You two have been an item from the start. That's it. Why didn't I see this? I mean I did see it, but I thought nothing of it. You were just as attracted to me as I was to you."

Tilting her head back, she laughed a laugh quite like no other I had ever heard and said, "Attracted to you! Mike said you were an ass. Boy was he right. How could someone who looks like me, be attracted to someone like you? You can never ever prove anything you silly piece of slime." Suddenly the southern accent disappeared and was replaced by a harsh tone, "Look at you. What are you anyway fifty? Fifty-one? Who in their right mind would be interested in a red-headed, freckled faced freak like you!"

I took a step back as if I had just been smacked in the face. Holding back my emotions that now were only hateful toward this woman of such inner ugliness, I felt my eyes suddenly well up. And before I had a chance to let a tear stream down my face, she did the unthinkable. Since the temperature was warmer than normal, Vicky too, had not worn a jacket. With a look of madness in her once tantalizing blue eyes, Vicky ripped at the shoulder of her blouse and tore the corner. She then took her own hand and slapped her face a few times in a row. A welt of finger marks instantly appeared. None of the few people on the street, at that moment, seemed to be paying attention to this spectacle of a scene. Bewildered as to why she just did what she did, I stood dead in my tracks speechless. Vicky, however, had more to say as she leaned in close to my ear as she had so many times in the past. This time her tone, of pure hatred, was different as she blurted out what I never could have imagined possible, even in my wildest dreams, "Listen to me Howdy Doody. Once I get to the office and tell them what you did to me, everyone and their mother will come looking for you. You will have no place to hide. You see, I knew the moment I saw you, that sucker was written all over your beet red face. I devised a plan immediately and then while I considered my options, I fell in love with Mike. I let him in on it all. All the while your silly little ass continued to drool over me. How easy was that? I couldn't have planned it better myself, without asking you to do the dirty work for me. I'll tell them all, that you did it all in hopes of winning me over. You waited for me this morning and confessed to me just what you did. Then you told me that you loved me, and wanted to take me away with you, and when I resisted, you attacked me. You bribed me with dirty money and I refused. You ripped at my blouse and started to beat me. I'm lucky to have escaped you with just these minor bruises." Once again in her best southern charmed voice, she continued "After all, no one will ever doubt the likes of a sweet ole southern girl like yours truly. You see, after I get done with ya all, your sorry little ass will wind up where it belongs. In prison. And Mike and I can enjoy the rewards that you worked so hard for. To think that such a weak fool like yourself, could make my man feel so inadequate. Now look who's gonna pay."

Shocked beyond belief, I took a step back and all at once, I was pushed to the ground. Out of nowhere two hands sent me flying to the pavement. Stopping the fall with the palm of my hands, I still landed hard enough to rip my pants leg in the knee. Blood instantly started to appear from the hole. And it hurt like hell. I turned around and who did I see. Mike Sullivan, who must have circled around the block, to sneak up and surprise attack me. What did I ever do to these two people to deserve this. Glaring down at me on the ground, he took hold of Vicky by the shoulders. "I witnessed the whole thing baby! Are you okay? Did that scumbag hurt you?", laughed Mike knowing all along what she did to herself. "I would really rough him up, but I don't want to give him any sympathy from the police when they whisk him the hell out of here. See, shithead. Payback isn't what your thought it would be. I got it all now. The girl, the money, and probably your title too! Poor little Howdy Doody. I guess it really is Howdy Doody time now. Together they laughed out loud, while I lay on the ground in tears. As I started to move back along the pavement on my butt to get away from them, I looked down for a second. And in the blink of an eye they were gone, leaving me all alone to absorb what I just heard and felt. Stolen money, a relationship with a man I despised, and false accusations of an attack. I was doomed. If I returned to my apartment I was certain police would be waiting to arrest me. Mr. Wilson would press charges against me as well. My life was over. I had nowhere or anyone to turn to. What was to be my milestone fiftieth birthday today, was now a living nightmare. Frightened, scared, uncertain of what the future now held, I thought of only one place that had always brought me peace and comfort. Perhaps if I headed there, I could sort things out and prove my innocence in this whole ordeal. Knowing I was wasting my time and it would be only hours before I was tracked down, I ran in full panic. I took off in the direction of Coney Island and all the wonders of that great big wheel.

56

With only the clothes on my back and a bit of cash in my pocket, I broke out in a sweat as I ran for the subway station. I took the flight of stairs as if I were being chased by a crowd of angry villagers. Fortunately for me a train had just pulled in and I immediately boarded it. Since I was heading away from the city, there were plenty of seats available in my car. Beads of perspiration were dripping from my forehead. I felt all eyes on me as if everyone knew I was some sort of criminal on the run. Paranoia was getting the best of me. I needed to get to the only place that would provide me with piece of mind, while I sorted this whole debacle out. My heart was beating so fast, it felt like it would explode out of my chest, at any given moment. I actually welcomed a heart attack to put me out of my misery. Even my knee continued to throb from Mike's push. My life was over. I had no place to go before they would find me. Even the sanctuary of the Wonder Wheel could only last so long. I bowed my head and started to pray. I asked our Heavenly Father, the Blessed Mother and Beloved Jesus to help get me out of this mess.

Suddenly the train came to a halt in the middle of the tunnel and all at once, the conductor came over the loud speaker. For no apparent reason the switches shut down and the central hub was working on getting the train up and running shortly. I figured my luck had something to do with this since quite frankly, it was running out. The few other passengers in the car started to complain out loud. Some were going to be late for an appointment, others were just annoyed at the situation at hand. I took a moment to bow my head again. While I had been at my wits end and deep in prayer to all of our Godly influences, the train stopped. How weird was that? As a few minutes passed, one agitated man came over to me and kicked my foot out of his way. I ignored him in hopes that I could avoid any more trouble. Sensing that he would get no response from me, the ticked off passenger left the car to head to another in search of a fight. As I watched him go between the two cars of the train, all at once he vanished into the next car. Instantly a new figure appeared. Wiping my eyes with both my hands, I stared at the figure. I knew I had seen that person before. I couldn't place my finger on when or where or even how long ago for that matter. Standing between the cars, the door to our train miracously opened on its own. It was at that precise second that I got a full view of the person. He wore a long black trench coat and his full head of wavy brown hair flowed as it had many years ago. His blue eyes were still as piercing and entered my soul as I continued to look. The figure didn't flinch or move. He lifted his hands up as if to call me to him. All the while I continued to gape in wonder. I couldn't budge. I felt paralyzed too. And as fast as he appeared, the man seemed to glaze over, until all that was left, was a blur in my eyes. Instantly, the train came to life and within minutes it pulled into the stop at Coney Island. Adding only more confusion to my life, I darted from the train. All the while, while I ran the few short blocks to the pier, I kept seeing his image in my head. How could it be possible? After all I hadn't seen or even thought of that person in years. Why now? The last thing I needed was a complete stranger to reappear at my most desperate time. And he hadn't even aged a bit. With the Wonder Wheel only a short distance off, I continued running. With a mind that was now surely mad, I reached my destination. My final destination.

57

Approaching the park, I headed in the direction of the Wonder Wheel. Since it was still morning, most of the rides hadn't opened yet. With a shortness of breath, I went to the ticket booth and bought my ticket. You see, as I ran, I thought of all the people that would really care if I existed or not, and couldn't think of one. Not a single person. I barely touched the lives of anyone. Therefore, I would rather die before spending my remaining years behind bars, for a crime I never committed. The ticket booth clerk stared at me as she passed me the ticket through the plexiglass opening. Again I felt like a fugitive on the run for something I didn't do. Eager to get on line and in my own car of the Ferris wheel, I dodged past the few people at the park to the line. Oddly enough, there was only one couple on line. A young couple perhaps in their twenties. As I was in deep despair, I couldn't help overhearing bits and pieces of their conversation. The young lady, who appeared to be from an upper class circle, was pleading with the young man, who looked like a real tough guy. Just by the clothes he was wearing you could see the class difference. She was in a pleated black and white skirt with a white sweater draped over her tan shirt. He, in torn dungarees and a black leather jacket over a t-shirt. He looked like a punk. To top it off, from above his jacket collar on his neck, was a tattoo of a snake. The head of a cobra was clearly visibly. The only people I knew, who sported tattoos, were either thugs or punks. The young girl was asking him to understand, that it would only be for three years. She would be home for holidays and breaks. Just like they were home now on spring break together. He insisted it would be different with her away in another state and all. I gathered she was going away to college. The discussion continued with her insisting he should be able to trust her while she was away. He wasn't buying her story for whatever reason and swore he would make her pay if she left him. He threatened that if he found out her parents were behind this, the outcome would be horrible. He also said that if he can't have her all to himself, nobody else would. I didn't like the way this conversation was heading, but I ignored it the best I could. Twice the young girl looked at me. I even noticed her briefly stare at my torn pant leg, which was now stained with dried blood. Not wanting to make eye contact, I stared down at the pavement. The last thing I needed was to get in the middle of a lover's quarrel. The ride operator opened their door to the car and they stepped into it. But not before the young girl with the big brown doe eyes, glanced one last time at me with fear in her eyes. I, again, looked the other way. They would have to work out their differences and come up with a plan that suited them best. After all, I had plans of my own.

58

I handed my ticket to the operator and prayed for a stationary car rather than the ones that ran the tracks inside the wheel. For once my prayer was answered. Ironically enough, both the last car with the young quarreling couple was as well stationary. I sat down as the wheel began to turn upwards to the best view of the world from the top. Once, then twice it went around. As it circled the second time, the line below started to fill up with excited patrons, who also wanted the thrill of the wheel. On the third and final time around the wheel, it continuously would stop to board other riders. Knowing I didn't have much time, if I was going to do what I had decided was my only option, I made my move. Quickly, I reached out and took hold of one of the steel beams. The young couple in the car above me had stopped at the tippy top. I was right beneath them. From this height I knew an immediate death would occur from this plunge I was about to partake. Inching my body through the cast iron metal car, I wedged myself where I was able to get a good grip and hauled myself up. Steadily I hoisted my entire body the rest of the way.

My knee throbbed but it was manageable. The pain had let up. With completely empty cars surrounding me, there was no one to take notice of the crazed man that I had become. There would be no screams to warn the operator on the ground. I stood on the flat top of my car peering out for the last time. Thinking that there was no other choice but this, I took a small step closer to the edge. Knowing that I wouldn't be able to convince authorities of my innocence, I had no other option. I really had no purpose in life. I wouldn't be missed. I made no impact in this world. My so called life had fallen apart. Sooner or later, the police would catch up with me and take me away in handcuffs. I couldn't let that happen. I started to lean forward, and just as I was about to take my final step, a strong gust of wind came out of nowhere and crashed into me. Instead of helping push me in the direction I needed to complete my destiny, it sent me flying backward. The scraped and bruised knee, gave out. Unable to catch my balance, I was reeling toward the other side. This wasn't supposed to happen like this. I needed to be in control of my final drop to the earth. Frightened of going over the side backwards, I tried in vain to grab hold of anything. I didn't want to die like this. In fact, I didn't want to die after all. I should fight the charges and prove it was Vicky and Mike and not me. Stand up for myself once and for all. Face the demons who wanted to drag me into the depths of hell. I want to LIVE! I'm an innocent man and I will stop at nothing, until every last person is convinced of my innocence. Desperately wanting to live now, once again I tried in vain to catch my footing, when the car tipped, knocking me back, smashing my head on a metal girder, leaving me unconscious.

59

What the heck just happened? Gradually, I began to sit up. Instead of being on top of the Wonder Wheel, I was in a forest. A forest so vast that all I saw were hundreds upon hundreds of oak trees. I scratched the top of my head. Actually, I felt the back of my head too, where I was certain a bump of an enormous size should be, from where it hit the steel beam. There was no bump or lump of any proportion. Nothing was there. How could this be? I know where I was and what I was about to do, before my change of heart. Then out of nowhere came that strong wind which knocked me off balance. Wait, my knee! My badly scraped knee and my torn pant leg. I looked down and there was no rip in my pants. No remnants of dried blood. I pulled up the pants and no cut of any sort.

What was going on? Nothing was making any sense to me. I stood up slowly figuring I may get dizzy from the bang on my head only seconds ago. Even my legs felt good. In fact, I felt fine. No, I felt better than fine. I felt great. Wonderful! I inhaled and felt the fresh air enter my lungs. Such tasteful oxygen graced my ribcage as I sucked it in. Fully refreshed and with a clear head, I surveyed my present surroundings. Beautiful oak trees of various sizes encircled me. Oak trees are not very tall at all. They are full bodied smaller trees with enormous amounts of leaves covering them. The top of the oak tree is huge compared to the base. Almost all of the leaves were shades of a light orange with tinges of brown and red. It reminded me of fall, right before autumn leaves would fall to make way for winter. I started to walk forward with no particular path in mind. Still reeling from being on top of the Wonder Wheel just moments ago to here now, baffled me. Then it hit me. All at once it hit me! I died. I mean I was dead. I didn't just fall back and hit my head. I ACTUALLY fell over the top of that car and splat. I started to rub my arms and then my legs to make sure they were mine. All was intact and as it should be. Again, nothing was making sense. I started to panic. From just a brief moment ago of taking fresh breathes, I now found it hard to catch my breath. I'm dead, oh my God I'm dead. Really dead. But I WANTED to live. I wanted to bring justice to myself and show the world who the enemy really was. With no real direction to run, I broke out in a fast stride. Weaving my way in between dozens of oak trees, I ran for a considerable amount of time before stopping. Leaning over with both my hands on my knees, I looked straight ahead. And what did my eyes rest on. Hundreds and hundreds more oak trees.

Endless oak trees. I was starting to freak out. Then out of thin air, I heard a voice speak.

"My child, why have you forsaken me?" Child, forsaken? What did I just hear? Again came the same soft voice but a bit louder, "My child, why have you forsaken me?"

Child, I'm a grown man who just turned fifty. Then realizing I was thinking to myself, I answered out loud, "There is no child here. In fact I turned . . . ." The voice cut me off and finished my sentence for me.

"Fifty today, my child."

"Whoa, who are you? What the heck is going on? Am I dead?"

"Relax my child, all in time. All in time."

"Please, I'm freaking out here! Where are you? Who are you? What am I doing here? Please help me."

"My child. I will answer all your questions, but for now relax. Take in all the beautiful scenery."

Scenery. All I saw were endless oaks full of leaves the color of autumn. Who was this voice and where was it coming from? It sounded like it was coming from the big, puffy, white clouds floating so leisurely through perfectly crystal clear blue skies. The voice from above stopped. Complete silence. Stunned, I waited for it to begin. I couldn't hear a thing. I dared not move in case the voice would return to this exact location. I stood still for minutes. When I finally determined that the voice had gone mute, I began to walk. Walking aimlessly among now thousands of these beautifully colored oak trees. The voice was right. I had never seen such beauty in a tree. Come to think of it, trees never really did catch my eye. As I continued what I now considered a stroll, I casually brushed my hand along the different textures of each tree. Each oak had a different feel to it. I found my legs start to pick up speed. I felt like a child, as I let my fingertips graze over each oak tree, and ran laughing through the forest of mighty oaks. Exhausted from running and belly laughing, I stopped in my tracks. The voice called me a child and that is exactly how I'm acting. How odd I thought. Suddenly, I noticed I was now in the middle of a large circle, with all the finest of oak trees around me. With arms fully extended, I twirled round and round as if I could take off from the ground. What was going on with me? Without a care in the world at that moment, I continued. Spinning around so fast, I became dizzy and fell to the ground, drained from the effort. As I sat with my butt on the grass, I heard a slight rustle of leaves. Then a bit louder rustle of leaves. I looked around at all the oak trees. Every tree had its leaves of various colors being swept off them. Magically, every leaf blew into a huge cloud that floated toward me. Although the noise of the rustling leaves grew louder, it felt so serene. Every oak tree that my eye could see was now bare. All of the leaves were gathered in this prism. Above and ahead of me, I continued to look directly at the middle of the massive amount of leaves. As I tried to focus on a group of leaves, an image appeared in the center. It was that guy with the long black hooded trench coat. Amidst the group of swirling leaves his wavy brown hair blew. He stood there and stared back at me with eyes the color of the ocean.

I was thrilled to see him again after our brief encounter in the subway.

Afraid he might instantly disappear I yelled, "PLEASE! who are you? Why over the course of my life do you appear and disappear so quickly? Answer me! Why am I here?"

A voice of greater strength spoke, "My child, why have you so often forsaken me?"

"Forsaken? What are you talking about? Please, talk to me. Like you did that time at the piers, between the tents. Don't leave me here. I don't know what is going on."

"My son. I am here, there and everywhere. I always have been here, but you have been blinded most of your life. I appear when you walk unsure."

The wind picked up and the leaves were whipping at lightning speed. As I tried to call out to the man within the leaves, his image faded. The circle of leaves were descending to the ground. Actually, the great ball of leaves, were entering the earth.

Angry that he left me again I screamed, "Come back! Don't leave me here alone! Come back!" Slowly the circle began to go under the grass just feet from where I now stood. It looked like a sunset that goes beneath the water of the ocean. Fearful of what lie in that circle, but afraid to stay behind, I dove head first into the great mass of Oak leaves. Certain, my head would hit the grass, I braced myself. I was awaiting impact. But impact never arrived. I floated among the leaves for what felt like an eternity. Tumbling head over heels among all those leaves, until I hit the bottom of a sand pit. Soft sand that felt all too familiar.

60

I landed face first in the sand. No, more like beach sand. I jumped up uncertain of where I was and what was happening. Covered in sand, I brushed off my body. I felt heat. Hot summer heat beating down on me. Looking around I was standing a couple of yards from the shoreline. I was alone on this vast beach. I walked down toward the shoreline. The temperature was getting warmer and I felt myself begin to sweat. I bent down and took off my shoes and rolled up my pants. I entered the ocean up to my calves. Since I was never an avid swimmer, I ventured no further. The water felt cool between my toes. Although the sun still beat down on me, my body was cooling off. I walked along this beach for hours, absorbing all its beauty. The sun that reflected off the white sand picked up other colors. Grains of pink and black mixed within the white creating a sand truly beautiful to behold. As I stared down at the tiny grains of sand I heard a splash from behind me. A good five hundred feet out in the water appeared a dolphin. A blue-finned dolphin. Larger than life, it sailed up out of the water and back beneath its surface. For as long as I could remember, I loved dolphins. Even as a kid, my mother when telling me a bedtime story, would often incorporate a dolphin into each tale. Whether it involved kings of great wealth in castles, or witches hidden in the woods, my mom always had a dolphin appear. In the moat that surrounded the castle, to the lake where the witch would gather water for her brew a dolphin would be present. I came to love dolphins more and more. That was why I found it so strange that one of such great beauty, now made its way toward me. The blue-finned dolphin slowly jumped up out of the water again and back under. It was headed straight for me. With the distance at twenty feet of water separating us, it jumped higher than it previously had. Before its descent into the ocean, it twirled around four times and splashed beneath. Astonished, I waited for it to reappear. It was just then that I heard a tiny splash to my right closer to the shore. Looking over I saw footprints in the sand. Since I was now almost knee deep in the water, I knew they didn't belong to me. I left the coolness of the water to see how this was possible. As I looked back from where I came, I saw a path of bare feet imprints. Confused I squinted, and as far back as I could see, I saw them following in my direction. They stopped at the precise spot where I now stood on sand as if the dolphin that just vanished, had materialized into them. Again baffled, I turned to continue walking. When I looked ahead, there stood the man in the trench coat. Right in my path. I gasped. Then I spoke, "Who are you? How is it you keep showing up out of thin air and disappearing before we get to speak."

The man in the hooded trench coat with the long wavy brown hair answered, "My child you have a lot to learn. Perhaps we can stroll along the shore together."

"Really?" I gasped, as if I were a kid just told by his parents, he could stay up late and watch scary movies.

Standing side by side, I put my shoes back on, and we started to walk. As we walked, I noticed how quiet everything was. Even the roar of the ocean sounded peaceful and serene to me. Looking over at this stranger, I watched how he moved. With such grace, as if he glided over the surface of the sand. The sun's beam, from only moments ago that beat down on me, felt refreshing to my skin.

As I stared, the stranger spoke again, "Jack, I wish all my people would appreciate the beauty of the world like you are experiencing now."

"How is it you know, my name?"

Smiling at what I assumed was my being so naive, the stranger continued, "Jack Rogan Reilly, born April 11th 1928. Faced a lot of trials and hardships along the way. Also the loss of loved ones over the years. Afraid to commit to a relationship, so chose to lead a quiet, isolated life. Until recently, when your world came tumbling down. Then ultimately deciding to end your life, but then a last minute change of heart."

"But how, why, do you know these things? Who are you?"

"I am you."

So confused I stopped walking and turned to face this stranger with eyes that bore into my soul, "You are me. What does that mean."

"I am you, him, her and everyone."

"But how? You are here with me now. There are no others with us."

"You see Jack. I am here with you now, because you need me the most. The others may need me later or summon me in prayer. Much like you did at your time of need. What you wanted to do to what is the most precious thing I and my Father have given you, was of utmost urgency. Life,

Jack, is the best gift given. You shouldn't feel that there was no other alternative. The air you breath to the emotions you feel are a gift. You could always taste, see, hear, smell and touch what other children of mine may not. Not all children are born perfect. You, Jack, were born perfect. You just never took the time to absorb all that life had given. Just as easily you were willing to give it up."

Listening to what he was telling me and inhaling every detail, we continued to walk off into the distance along the beach.

Thinking I had figured it all out I asked, "So I am dead. I did fall backward off the Wonder Wheel. This is MY heaven. An eternity by myself. What about the great white light at the end of the tunnel? All the ones I loved and cherished so dearly, waiting for me with open arms?"

And all at once it hit me like a ton of bricks. This stranger with the black hooded trench coat. No, this man with the curly brown hair and pointed nose. The guy with the piercing blue eyes that I worshipped every Sunday at church for most of my life. Even his beard and mustache should have told me who he was. It couldn't be. Burning bushes, parted seas, and stone tablets with thou shall nots were from centuries past. Not a living soul in almost the last two thousand years, had laid eyes on this great being. As steady as I could keep my quivering voice, I managed to say the only one word I could, "JESUS?"

As if I should have known all along who this fellow was and so nonchalantly he replied, "Yes, my son."

I felt both my knees give out, as I fell to the ground kneeling in front of him.

"Oh, Heavenly Father. Lord, God. Almighty Savior." I couldn't stop myself. I was babbling as I knelt in front of this great figure.

"Pick yourself up Jack. Let's continue our walk." And just like that I felt myself lift off the ground and continue to walk.

Jesus spoke first, "Why have you forsaken me Jack?"

"Forsaken, you Lord. I never, ever would or could have forsaken you."

"But at your most difficult crisis you prayed but you didn't pray. You pushed me away instead of inviting me in."

Not understanding, I asked, "You were there? Always!" I then remembered the strong wind that knocked me over.

"But you closed your heart to me and my Father. You let your faith fall short."

"No, I didn't have anywhere to go. No one to turn to."

"Yes, my son, I know. When you were down to nothing, I was up to something. Don't you see Jack. You have always been unsure. You journeyed alone, when I have always walked beside you."

"But how? Why me?"

"Like I said before, not just you Jack. All that believe. Whether they worship in my house or not. As long as they believe."

"But the Bible says you must worship in the House of the Lord."

"The Bible says a lot according to Luke, Matthew, John and my other followers. Revelations exist, but only to those who have it in their hearts to follow."

Trying to make sense of it all and most importantly that Jesus walked beside me, I questioned him again, "So, only good people have it in their hearts to do what is right. To lead a religious life. A sacrificing life. Is that what you mean?"

"I mean nothing Jack. You mean me."

"How?"

"By believing in the Father, the Son and the Holy Spirit. The Holy Trinity will give you eternal life. A life to live forever."

"Yeah, but if that were the case. What about my parents? They were very faithful, believing people and they were taken away from me at such young ages."

"Jack, no one is ever taken away. Their time on this earth was up and greater heavens awaited them. They walk with me. Now and always."

"But, I miss them. I loved them both very much. Are they together Jesus? Are they happy? I think about them both. My mother was my world. My father, according to my mother, adored me. Help me Jesus. I want to know they are with you in peace." Suddenly, the bright blue sky became brighter as the sun glowed its most yellow rays.

Our slow stride along the shoreline moved us more briskly ahead. Following a ray of light from the sky, I noticed two people who sat on a blanket in the sand. The light shone down on them, like a spotlight beam that shines upon an actress on a Broadway stage. Now floating, toward the couple, with my feet not touching the sand, we stopped fifteen feet from them. The woman was slicing a loaf of bread as the man poured them each a glass of red wine. After she placed cheese on each piece of their bread, she handed him his slice.

They clinked glasses, all the while smiling and staring into one another's eyes. Interlocking their one arm to eachother's other, like young lovers, they sipped the wine.

So much love was displayed on their faces. Starry eyed and compassionate toward one another, like star-crossed lovers. I instantly recognized who they were, from their wedding picture. My parents. My mother and father. Maeve and Seamus Reilly. Happy together forever. Eternally youthful, as they once were. Every day they would spend eternity picnicking on the beach if they chose to. Perhaps sailing on a Grand Luxury Liner around the world and back. Flying to the moon and back as man had done only a few short years ago. I now knew deep down within my heart, that together forever they would be. I called out to them, but my voice went unheard. I screamed out at the top of my lungs to no avail. I wasn't to be seen or heard. I was just a spectator looking in. Almost as if they were inside a crystal ball. A looking glass. For a brief moment, I considered bee-lining straight to the source of light. I reconsidered and decided against it. I dare not get too close for fear I would shatter their eternal rest. However, I needed to be closer. Within a hands length. Seeing them like this became too much for me to bear and witness. I dropped to my knees and wept. I wept for the love they would always share. Then I cried. I cried like I never cried before. I missed them. Really missed them. There is no love greater that I had, than for these two people. My mother and father. Pulling myself together, I dried my eyes on my shirtsleeve. Forever grateful for this opportunity to see them at such peace, I turned to thank Jesus. Truly thank him. In the time I was staring and then weeping over my beloved parents, Jesus had made his way into the ocean. Fully clothed, he swam out to sea, leaving me behind once again. I couldn't let him leave. I still had so many questions, that I needed answered. Doubts that needed to be put to rest. He never even answered if I was dead or alive. I needed JESUS and I wasn't about to lose him again. Deciding I would follow him wherever it took me, I swam off after him. My face hit the unseasonably warm salt water first. Having never been taught to swim, I had no trouble keeping up with the current. Always leery of water, I now became an Olympic contender. Each stroke I took, brought me closer and closer to Jesus. After swimming for a considerable amount of time, Jesus still had a lead over me. I stopped and started to tread water, to get my bearings as to how far of a distance apart we were. The ocean water, which I had always imagined to be frigid, was relatively warm. No, actually it was hotter than I ever thought possible. Bobbing up and down as the waves took my body gently in each fold, I spotted Jesus. Just a few yards from me. Somehow, he slowed down. Right in front of him was an enormous whirlpool. The ocean had opened up and swirls of water were spinning within its eye. A giant abyss with a drain at the bottom. Tons and tons of this beautiful ocean water spun within its grasp. Jesus, having never glanced back, swam straight into the whirlpool and was sucked underneath. Knowing I would never be able to hold my breath with gallons of water pouring in my mouth, I proceeded to swim right to the eye. I was no longer afraid. And as I reached the rim to suddenly be sucked beneath, I heard a voice in my head. It was Jesus' voice and it was telling me; 'Be not afraid, I go before you always. Come follow me.' And follow him I did, as I was plunged into the unknown.

61

"Watch your step Jack! Stay ON the rocks. Away from the ones with moss!

Be careful my son. We still have much for you to see."

Completely dry and standing atop a small boulder situated in a line with other rocks of different sizes, I kept my balance. Somehow I surfaced out of the whirlpool, and stood by the most wondrous waterfall I'd ever seen.

Cascading down from where I stood on the rock, it sounded thunderous. Splashes of water from the falls, covered my entire body, drenching me from head to toe. It was exhilarating from the spray. Off to the side of the falls blossomed thousands upon thousands of various flowers. Exotic, tropical and standard types that come around only during Spring. African Moon, Alpine Aster, Morning Glory, and Pussy Willows too beautiful for the human eye. Roses, Orchids, Crocus, and daffodils of the utmost beauty as well. Taking in a deep breath, I smelled fragrances that enriched my senses; the aromas so invigorating. Looking ahead, the line of rocks stretched from one side of the falls across to the other. I was almost directly in the middle. I leaned forward to peer over the edge and couldn't believe the drop. Having seen Niagara Falls in books and on the PBS station about its history, this waterfall was twice its size in comparison. Carefully I leaned back. Rushing water spilled over its edge. If I had fallen into the water, I would be sent flying over the falls. It would be an instant death as my body would be splattered upon the rocks below. Just then, I realized what Jesus was telling me. To be careful not to slip. Which would mean that if I slipped, I would die. And if I died, I wouldn't be alive like I was now. So I was alive after all. But how?

Was I dreaming all this? I smacked my cheek lightly to wake myself up, if I were indeed sleeping. Nothing. I was still in the same spot on the same rock. Jesus must have been watching because he spoke up, "Jack, why are you doubting your being here with me? This isn't a dream. This is to make you see all that I and my Father have given you and what you will give back in return."

Confused over his last statement, I questioned, "What DO I have to offer in return? What is my purpose? You see Jesus, I have nothing but a life behind bars waiting for me.

Unless I can prove my innocence, I will be sent directly to jail for a crime I didn't commit. How does that benefit my religious well-being?"

Jesus who had been off to the side, simultaneously appeared on the rock next to mine.

His arms started to move in a clockwise circle. The cascading waterfall in all its beauty, formed a screen within its center. The rushing water parted to make room for a huge screen the size of a drive-in movie. Blurry figures started to take shape within the water on the screen.

Jesus spoke, "Pay attention to what you are about to see. You see Jack, things were already in the works before this morning when you thought your life was over."

Peering into the waterfall, images now formed. I rubbed my eyes to make sure I was seeing who I thought I was seeing. All alone and sitting in a pew at a Church was Mr. Wilson. He was in the first pew closest to the altar. The church was completely empty except for him. It looked as if he was deep in prayer. Often I would sit in the same position as he and pray just like he was doing.

"What is Mr. Wilson doing?" I asked. Then I answered my own question, "I often pray as he is doing right now. You see Jesus, I believe one MUST go to Church. You, however, stated that others could pray anywhere as long as they pray. The Church is my outlet and I am its plug. Each and every week I plug myself in, so that I can recharge my faith. A faith to get me through the next week. Not being in the House of the Lord is cheating. If you can't spare an hour each week, then you're only cheating yourself."

"Jack, my dear Jack. You aren't cheating if you worship outside my house. As long as you believe in God is all that really matters. As long as I am thought about each and every day in someones mind is enough to sustain my being."

"I don't understand. I think about you every Sunday and know that you are taking care of my parents and even Father Bill. For that only I am thankful."

"But you've still forsaken me, Jack."

"Forsaken, how?"

"By not truly believing that I was with you. Always with you. At your side."

"But . . . ."

"Watch and see. Look into the water and witness for yourself."

"Nothing is making sense."

"Watch my son, watch."

I peered again into the water. Mr. Wilson was still praying. Heavily praying as if looking for answers. Then he faded. Faded into a blur again only to be replaced by images I cared not to see. I almost lost my footing by who appeared next and stuck my arms out at my sides to catch my balance. Vicky Hillbrandt and Mike Sullivan were outside of some sort of disco waiting behind velvet ropes. A big burly bouncer pointed to them and opened the rope to let them in. As they passed by I noticed overhead a sign that read Studio 54. Studio 54 was the hottest discotheque since it opened its doors just a year prior in 1977. Celebrities from near and far frequented this hot spot. Rushing in, they immediately found their way to the bar. Drinks and shots were consumed by both Vicky and Mike as they then danced the night away. The water rinsed over the screen and again there were the two of them. This time they were in a restaurant having a candle light dinner. They had just given their order to the waiter, who was dressed in a black tuxedo with white gloves. As he took their menus, I noticed it read Tavern on the Green, a fancy well do to restaurant that had opened back during the depression in 1934. Fading just as fast and bringing them back into focus for the third time, they were again making their way to an elevator bank. Mike pressed the up button and they entered the elevator. Once inside, he hit the button that showed Windows of the World on the 107th floor of the North Tower of the World Trade Center. Why was I being shown all these ritzy places? I couldn't figure out the reason, but I continued to stare as I felt like a captivated audience waiting for the next scene. No sooner and the images disappeared and reappeared. Mike was laying in a bed in his boxer shorts while Vicky stood over him in a red negligee. He was tossing up wads of bills into the air as the bills slowly floated down onto the bed. Together they laughed. Then Vicky laid down next to him on top of the bills and rolled over to face him. Mike leaned into her where he passionately started to kiss her. My eyes had seen enough and I turned away before I would see more than I cared to.

Watching me cover my eyes Jesus whispered, "It's okay, Jack. They're gone. Keep looking. You WILL be pleased by what you see next."

I peeked between my finger as kids often do when they don't want to see something. Jesus was right, not that I should have doubted him. I just couldn't let myself look at them like that.

As I stared mesmerized into the water of the falls again, Mr. Wilson reappeared. This time he was in his office. His secretary, Irene, was there too. Together they looked like they were scrutinizing some ledgers. She busy with a calculator, and he with pencil and paper. Moments later, two well-dressed men in business suits entered and flashed some sort of credentials to prove their ID. Words were exchanged back and forth among the four of them. Then they walked over to Vicky and Mikes desks and rummaged through them and their drawers. I was totally confused now. Until all at once the water rippled like it never had. What I saw next blew my mind. Could it be? Was this really happening? Mr. Wilson and some of his staff were waiting in the lobby along with those two gentlemen in the suits. Also present were two uniformed police officers too. The revolving doors spun and there entered Vicky and Mike. I could see she was wearing the torn blouse and her face was still swollen from her own handiwork. Instantly their smiles disappeared. A look of surprise crossed both their faces, but not before the two policemen turned them around and handcuffed them both. The two suited gentlemen were speaking to them. I was highly upset that all the dialogues were silent, as I couldn't hear what anyone was saying in any of the images I'd seen. The screen now faded too, and the rush of water again replaced where it had just been.

"So what does this all mean? Why am I watching all this? What exactly is happening to them?"

I wanted an answer this time and my voice was more determined in asking, "I need to know Jesus. Why show me Mr. Wilson and then Vicky and Mike. Please, at least tell me what it all meant."

Jesus, in his hooded trench coat, looked lovingly at me and said, "Mr. Wilson is a smart man Jack. With age comes wisdom. A few weeks after Vicky started, he began to distrust her. The way she made certain moves around you and then secretly around Mike, raised a red flag. Mr. Wilson hired a private investigator to follow Vicky over the next couple of weeks. The private investigator had taken many pictures of her late night outings. Mr. Wilson knew there was no possible way on her salary, she could visit those restaurants and nightclubs and spend that type of cash. When his intuition proved him correct, and also from the photos provided by the investigator, he devised his own plan. Although he sacrificed you in front of the whole office, it was never his intent to hurt you for very long. He had every intention of letting you know the very next day of the final outcome. That was until you met up with Vicky on your own. Shortly after you took off to Coney Island, they reached the office and that is what you just saw. Vicky never did get the chance to blame you with her fake story. Mr. Wilson beat them at their own game. Their plan to swindle all that money and get away with it was over. Mr. Wilson had enough proof to put them both behind bars, for a very long time. You, Jack, chose to take a different route all together."

"But I didn't! I mean I did at first, but then I changed my mind. I was going to FIGHT back. I swear to it I was."

"I don't need you to swear Jack. I know what you were thinking each and every moment.

That is why I became the wind. To give you the push you needed. A push in the other direction. A direction to make you believe in yourself again.

I, like I have told you often, walk beside you and within you. If you would have given it some more thought and a bit of more time, the end result would be different all around. You see, Jack. This is all still the same day. You are frozen in time. You need to believe again. Truly believe in not only me, my Father and your faith. But in yourself. You do indeed have a purpose. One that is still many years away. Now come with me, my son. Be not afraid and take my hand."

I was ashamed again for doubting my faith and my belief in Jesus. What was wrong with me. Here he stood all this time convincing me of who I was, yet I was afraid. Afraid to take that greatest challenge. To truly believe in ME!

Then he did what I feared most. Jesus stepped off the rock and literally hung over the steep drop of the falls. He extended his one hand out to me, wanting me to take it. I was petrified and didn't take hold of it at first.

"My son, Jack. Again you doubt me. Take that first step and the rest will fall into place. Fear of the unknown will never occur when you are with me. Now come Jack, come."

Now, unafraid with the presence of Jesus with me, I let my one foot leave the rock. And just like that, altogether at once with the other foot, I stepped off the safety of my rock. Quickly I grabbed his hand in mine. Dangling hundreds of feet above the earth, while the waterfall continued to flow beneath us, I did not pummel to the rocks below. I stood hand in hand with my savior Jesus Christ. Together, we walked directly into the pulsating water of the falls. Never to be frightened again, I took my biggest leap of faith ever, as I followed Jesus through the falls to what lay ahead.

62

After, what felt like a brief second, we passed through the water. And once again, I found myself alone. This time I was standing in what I estimated to be about two inches of the purest snow. Snow so white it blinded my eyes. I waited as my eyes adjusted to the glare of the whiteness. Dressed in only a light shirt and dress pants, I should have been shivering from the cold. My breath produced winter frost from my mouth, but I wasn't the slightest bit chilled. I should have been freezing with all this snow surrounding me. However, I wasn't. For as far as the naked eye could see, the surface was completely snow covered. There was just me and miles of this land filled with snow. Nothing, but flat ground and acres of snow. No trees, grass, rocks or anything. Just snow. I inched my feet through it making a small patch of snow into a pile in front of me. What I saw, as the snow cleared from where my feet were, totally surprised me. Quickly, I started to push and brush the snow away with my shoes. Beneath my feet was ice. Solid ice. Stomping my feet, the ice felt harder than a rock. Now in a frenzy, I cleared away a small circle. From the looks of it, I was standing on complete ice. A lake of water larger then I could imagine. As I started to clear more of the snow, all at once, a wind arose from behind me. Turning to face the breeze, I noticed that quite a large amount of snow was lifting up off the ice. Floating upward toward the heavens, swirls of white powder rose. The wind swept around in a full motion until a large area had been cleared. It was now a sheet of ice surrounding me. Perhaps a dozen feet away, I caught a glimpse of something unusual. There out of the ice, came a head covered in long wavy brown hair. As the figure slowly emerged up out of the depths of the frigid waters below, I immediately knew who it was. Jesus, my Blessed Savior, had risen up completely out of the frozen solid ice. Dressed as he always was, his clothes were dry. His trench coat should have been soaked. Approaching me, he spoke, "Jack, we have come as far as we can. Your journey is almost complete with me."

"No, Jesus, no! I want to stay here with you forever. I want to be one of your Apostles."

"My son, you have so much more to accomplish before that time."

"Please, don't you get it! I will follow you always. Like you told me before. Let me do this, please," I pleaded.

With only sincerity in his voice, he beckoned me to come closer, "Come Jack. See all that you must see."

Walking to where he stood, I was told to look beneath my feet. Where there was only water now cleared to host thousands of endless activities taking place beneath me.

"Look at all the images, Jack. Absorb what you see. Really absorb every last detail."

I knelt down to get a better view beneath the ice. Pools of dolphins swam alongside sharks. Polar bears lifted seals up out of air, and playfully tossed them into the ocean.

Fierce piranhas swam peacefully among all types of fish. Confused, I looked up at Jesus.

"Keep watching Jack. Keep absorbing it all."

Again, I peered down. Now there were rows of identical houses lined up next to one another. Blocks and blocks of homes lined the streets. Standing on their front lawns in conversations with one another, as neighbors often do, were races of every color. Caucasians, African Americans, Hispanics and Asians to name a few. They were laughing and happily living among each other.

Now crawling on all fours, I moved along to see what else was beneath the waters.

A large gathering of people were standing together. A stage was set up before the huge turnout of spectators. At a podium stood a woman, while the American Flag appeared to her right. She patiently waited as the audience applauded. Behind her were a dozen or more chairs. Dignitaries from every country and nation sat in the seats. Countries that were once not our allies shared space among us. Germany, Russia, China, Cuba and even Vietnam diplomats were present cheering with the crowd. The picture was so surreal. All those countries that we, at one time went to war with, all gathered together. This woman, whose presence seemed to make a difference, had the whole world in perfect harmony.

Who she was, I had no inkling. I was baffled when I asked, "Who is she Jesus? What is going on?"

Jesus answered, "What do you think my son is going on?"

"I don't know. I mean sharks with dolphins, blacks and whites living next door to one another. What is the world coming to?"

"You already know the answer Jack. Think within and you will know."

"But all that doesn't make sense. Like perfect harmony or something. As if Harmony is and always will be the answer." Then it dawned on me. What I was seeing was the future. Everything I witnessed beneath the surface was a glimpse of what lie ahead for us as a world; living together in perfect harmony. With harmony, came peace and tranquility.

"Exactly, Jack!"

I was just about to ask him exactly what when I realized, he had heard my thoughts before I spoke them. I stood up and faced him.

"But where do I fit in? I mean why do I need to see all this? Who is that woman? Some sort of political figure I'm assuming. How does she fit into MY life?"

"Enough my son. All in time. You have experienced all you need for now. It is time."

"Time?" I asked.

"Yes, Jack. You are ready to return to all that was yours."

Panicked and with fear starting to grip me again, I said "No, Jesus! Don't you see. I'm not ready." I took a deep breath and all at once, I realized what his message was. I put my fears behind me as I thought. As long as Jesus was with me. By that I mean within my heart and soul, I shall not be afraid. Calming down as fast as the fear had gripped me, I felt at peace. Truly at peace. How many men could walk with Jesus. Through my savior, I witnessed my life. All that was given to me and all that was to come. I would cherish each and every day from this moment on. With a true enlightment to my being, I knew I had a purpose. In time all would tell. But for now I would live each day to its fullest. With a single question left, I asked "Jesus, when will I walk with you again?"

Smiling with the most beautiful smile I had and would ever see again, he answered, "I will wait for you with open arms when your time has come. For now, go back Jack. And live. Really live."

I went to hug and thank him, and just as I leaned into him, he disappeared. Vanished into thin air. I LOVED Jesus. I really loved him and would each and every day of my existence. How I would make this up to him, I would never know. Like Jesus had told me just moments ago, in time, all in Time. I fell to the ground crying hysterically. Never before in my life had I wept like this. Exhausted, I cried myself to sleep. A sleep so comforting I thought I would never awaken.

63

Instantly, I was awakened by a loud scream. Where only seconds ago I lay upon ice, now it was cold metal. Jolted out of a peaceful slumber, I sat upright.

Disoriented and a bit groggy, I felt the back of my head. A lump the size of a walnut was present. Slowly, all that had happened began to come back to me filtered by my groggy state. I was on top of a car of the Wonder Wheel. Having second thoughts of jumping to my death, I lost my footing and must have been knocked out. I met Jesus. He was so real. Everything I had seen and felt, was so real. And as I started to remember all the seasons that I had witnessed with Jesus, I saw feet. Yes, feet, dangling from the car directly above me. Bare legs were attached to them. A full body came into view and I knew who it was. The young girl, who moments earlier, had been arguing with her boyfriend about going away to college. She was screaming as she held on for dear life. Her hands were clasped tightly on the bars that enclosed the car. Her boyfriend, with a deranged look upon his face, was shoving her through the open door. Her legs were swinging back and forth. She was pleading with him saying she couldn't hold on for much longer. She continued to beg him to pull her back up. He, on the other hand, ignored her frantic pleas and was trying to pry her fingers off the bars. He was cursing and screaming at her the whole while, as one by one he loosened each finger. People on the ground had now heard her screams for help. Many of the bystanders below were now pointing to the scene above, as it was unfolding. With little time to spare before this young girl fell to her certain death, I reacted. I jumped up on my feet and was greeted immediately by a sharp pain in my knee. Apparently the shove Mike had given me, had done some severe damage to it. Holding steady and biting my upper lip from the throbbing pain throughout my one leg, I inched closer to the edge of my car. Hoping her legs would swing one more time in my direction, I put both my arms out. The young girl's legs came into my grasp at the precise moment her last three fingers let go of the bars. Together, we toppled backwards and landed on our backs. Staring into her petrified eyes from the sheer terror she had just experienced, I felt some sort of instant connection. I felt like I had known this young girl my whole life, which, of course, wasn't the case. I also felt that from this point forward, we would share a bond for life.

64

As good fortune along with an Irish Blessing would have it, the brown eyed girl was named Marnie H. Jefferson. She was a direct descendant of Thomas Jefferson, our third President of the United States, on her father's side. Having come from a family of political background, she had just finished college and was to attend Harvard Law School in Cambridge, Massachusetts in the fall. Both her father and mother were born in Shadwell, Virginia as was Thomas Jefferson himself. Once out of college and after marrying his high school sweetheart, together they moved to affluent Greenwich, Connecticut. Matthew, her father, studied law and eventually opened a successful law practice on Park Avenue in Manhattan. Mimi, her mother, was a stay at home mom raising their three daughters, of which Marnie was the oldest. Mimi was on many fund-raising committees and actively involved in their local Church. Marnie, who wanted to make a difference in the world, followed in her father's footsteps. She vowed not to work in her father's firm so that she could establish a name of her own. Matthew's practice was corporate in nature, whereas Marnie wanted to put violent criminals behind bars for good. Like her grandfather, Thomas Jefferson, of many father's past, he started the movement to develop freedoms in America, hence the Declaration of Independence. Marnie wanted to continue to keep people safe and free from all harm. Unfortunately, while she was in her sophomore year at John Jay Criminal Justice College she met Kyle Adams, a kid from the wrong side of the tracks. Having been sent from foster home to foster home, he grew up to be a troubled teen. With the help of a devoted guidance counselor and vice-principal, he was able to get his life together to a certain degree, before graduating high school. On a full scholarship, due to his financial needs and good grades, he convinced the admissions board that he would make the college proud. However, shortly after the first few weeks, he fell in with the wrong crowd once again. Drugs and alcohol meant more to him than his education. In his freshman year he was almost asked to leave, but once again persuaded the right people to give him another chance. It was sophomore year, in a required class, that he met and fooled Marnie into believing they shared the same dreams. And all through their sophomore, junior and senior years they dated. For three years, Kyle used Marnie as a means to support his habits and to help him to pass his classes. Marnie, with all her heart, and knowing she was being used, believed she could change this man she now loved. Secretly she dated Kyle. Her parents had visited during an open house during her second year and when they met Kyle, they instantly disliked him. Matthew saw right through him and forbade his eldest daughter to see him. In order to see it through, he threatened to cut off her monthly allowance. Her parents were by no means snobs, but in their upper class status, the likes of Kyle was unacceptable. Marnie continued to see him over the years. However, over time Kyle became more abusive to her mentally and even physically a couple of times recently. Instead of going home for spring break her senior year, she stayed at school, telling her parents the school workload was just too much. The bruises on her arms from where Kyle would grab her and scream at her for even looking at another guy, would certainly catch her parent's eyes. Realizing that this man she no longer loved would never let her be, she decided to transfer to Harvard

Law School to finish her degree. Kyle's grades just weren't good enough and all the talking in the world, couldn't get him into Harvard. For that she was grateful. With all those miles between them, Marnie hoped he would find someone else and move on. She had supported him and his habits long enough, only to now be beaten by him. Kyle would be lucky if he could land any job let alone one in law. How she ever let herself wind up with someone like Kyle, she didn't know. What Marnie did know, was that it was people like him that made her want to lock up all the bad guys in the world for good. So today at Coney Island Amusement Park, she would break the news to him. Fooling him into believing she would wait for him, she practiced over and over what she would say. Marnie would tell him at the top of their favorite ride ever. The Wonder Wheel, where she and Kyle, even in their most stressed out times, felt relaxed.

Marnie smiled a real smile for the first time in years. Freedom was only months away. All she had to do now, was convince this guy she had grown to despise, that she was his forever. However, her forever was almost cut too short. Until, I, Jack Rogan Reilly, saved not only her life, but mine as well.

65

Total mayhem awaited us. No sooner had our car come fully around, the ride operator and several other park employees helped us off the top of the car. Two other tough looking ride operators grabbed hold of Marnie's delinquent boyfriend and held him until the police arrived. By this time the crowd that gathered was quite large. The policemen had within a few shorts minutes appeared on the scene. After taking Marnie and my statements, they handcuffed Kyle and placed him in their squad car. Marnie was most certainly pressing charges and with the eventual support from her parents, Kyle, the deranged ex-boyfriend, would spend a considerable amount of time locked away. If her father got his way, it would be for life. As the police car pulled away from what could have been a tragic event, the crowd applauded. I, too, turned to leave but immediately stopped. Marnie had asked me to wait with her, until both her parents arrived. While we waited, someone must have notified the news. Not even an hour had passed since we were helped off the car, and several news crews arrived. Reporters were pushing their way through the crowd with their cameramen close behind to get an exclusive first. Marnie did most of the talking, as I nodded my head mostly in agreement. Flashes went off and for a short time I was blinded by all the snaps from the cameras. Matthew and Mimi Jefferson finally arrived, after what felt like a lifetime, but was only two hours. Her parents thanked me and offered to give me a ride back to my apartment. I graciously accepted, since I was emotionally and physically drained from all that had happened. As the four of us left Coney Island for Manhattan, her father promised he would make this up to me. He was indebted to me for life. From the moment we were helped off the ride, I never once was asked why I was on top of my car of the Ferris wheel. Instead, I was deemed a hero. A real life hero that risked his life to save another. I made a promise to myself, that unless confronted to tell the truth, I would keep my secret. I would never offer an explanation either. Some things were better left unsaid. We finally arrived at my apartment as Mr. Jefferson pulled up to the curb. I was letting myself out of their car, when Marnie, who had been sitting next to me, leaned over and placed a peck on my cheek. I knew then, that this girl would never forget me.

Amid many heartfelt thanks from all three Jefferson's, I was glad that this whole ordeal was finally over. Hopefully, left behind for good. What I didn't realize, was that this was only the beginning of a new life for me.

66

The very next morning, a few of the other brownstone tenants gathered at my third floor front door to congratulate me. Dressed only in a robe covering my pajamas, I had slept fitfully. Now as hordes of accolades poured forth, someone showed me the headlines of the Daily News. Plastered across the front page was a photo of me and Marnie. The headline read, '**Wonderman saves Uptown girl from certain DEATH!**' I couldn't believe it. A picture of us sitting next to each other, both visibly shaken and physically exhausted, staring at one another. I quickly read the caption under our photo and I was being referred to as a super hero. Thanking my fellow apartment dwellers, I closed the door. I was in total disbelief. I was a hero. My whole life I floated under the radar and now I'm a hero. No sooner had I started to read the article from the front page, when my phone rang. I answered and it was a local television station asking to interview me with Marnie about our experience. The station manager said her father Matthew had lots of connections and he was certain more offers like this would be made. This man wanted first option on speaking with the two of us. I told him I would give it some serious thought and took his name and number and promised to be in touch. Not even thirty seconds later my phone rang again. It was another television station begging for an exclusive. Throughout the morning my phone continued to ring off the hook. Too tired to go over the whole conversation again, I decided to let the answering machine pick up. I sat in my small one room apartment, pondering just how far this could go. Listening but not really paying attention, I heard Mr. Wilson's voice come over the answering machine. I sprang up and grabbed the receiver. Mr. Wilson too, was congratulating me. In fact for the next hour he brought me up to date on what had taken place in my absence. The funny thing was, that as he spoke in great length and detail, I already knew what he was telling me. Hearing it all over again only confirmed my sentiments, that Jesus was not a dream, but indeed a reality.

67

After hanging up with Mr. Wilson and accepting his hundredth apology for what he did to me to cover up his plan, I lay back in my bed. Not only did he offer me my old job, but he wanted to speak with me about possibly becoming an investor with shares in his empire. He told me to take the rest of the week off to think about it. I couldn't believe how my life had suddenly turned around all in the blink of an eye. Just yesterday, my birthday, my life was in total ruins. Fast forward one day and my life was given back to me with things looking better and better. It took a second but then I realized exactly why it had. I believed. Truly believed. And nothing or no one would ever make me not believe. I needed to shower and dress and go to the one place where I was forever grateful. I wanted to sit in Church and thank God for my second chance at life. I needed quiet time to absorb all that had taken place in the last twenty-four hour time span.

Quickly, I finished getting myself up and out. As I left the brownstone in Greenwich Village, heading for the subway ride to Saint Patrick's Cathedral, I was so excited to praise Jesus. Unfortunately hundreds of people would detour me for hours, with praise for their new hero. Me.

68

People from every direction were pointing toward me shouting "That's him! The guy who saved that girl on the Ferris Wheel!" Others yelled, "Hey Wonderman, can we get your autograph?" Every place I seemed to dodge the onlookers, I would come face to face with more. With newspapers in hand, strangers felt like they knew me, because my picture was splattered across the front page. After all it isn't that hard to spot a grown man with bright red hair and freckles. Even at fifty, I still had no gray hairs. Curiosity seekers actually blocked my path in order to ask me questions such as, "How does it feel to be New York's Wonderman? Did the Uptown girl's wealthy parents give you a reward? Can you please sign my paper and address it to my son? He'll just love it!"

Question after rapid question too fast for me to even answer before being thrown another.

Not wanting to come across as impolite, I answered as many as I could, before maneuvering my body around the present crowd, into the throng of approaching people.

Again, I answered all the questions that had since been repeated over and over to me. Backing away from this new bunch of worshippers, I decided I needed some sort of disguise. Greenwich Village, with many interesting shops, made it easy to find a thrift store. I purchased a hat and dark sunglasses. The disguise actually worked. With my head down toward the pavement, I managed to get to the subway. Seated in the car, I sensed people were starting to recognize me again. They would glance down at their newspaper and back up to where I sat. With fingers crossed, I made it the few stops before getting off at Penn station at 34th Street and 7th Avenue. I walked at a quick pace toward 51st Street and Fifth Avenue. As I saw St. Patrick's Cathedral on the corner, I made my final stride toward my house of worship. I desperately needed this refuge. A shelter to take cover in, while this raging storm of instant fame passed over. Wonderman may be a hero in New York City, but Jack Rogan Reilly wasn't cut out to take over Manhattan.

69

I prayed the remainder of Wednesday afternoon. If you haven't ever been inside the cathedral it is absolutely breathtaking. Tourists from around the world visit this unique and exquisite church. It was built over one hundred years ago in 1879. The cathedral and associated buildings were declared a National Historic Landmark only two years prior in 1976. I always found a somewhat secluded area off to the side in the church to pray. On any given day or time, the church was crowded. If you were able to be with only a handful of people surrounding you, you were considered lucky. Silently I asked Jesus to guide me through this sudden notoriety gently. Knowing He now and always had walked with me, it would provide me with the strength to get past it. I thanked him for letting me see the light and to approach all life's punches head on. I could face any challenge with the spirit within my heart.

Deciding that I would return to work the very next day and talk with Mr. Wilson about a seat on his board, I knelt at the altar and made the sign of the cross. I counted my blessings for this second chance. A second chance to make a difference.

70

On Thursday morning bright and early, I walked into Wilson Textiles. Greeted as if I were a celebrity by everyone, I walked into Mr. Wilson's office. We talked again in great detail about what position I would hold, and just how many share options I now acquired.

His facial expression alone upon first seeing me, showed me just how delighted and pleased he was to have me return. So a mutual agreement was made, a bond rekindled, signatures affixed and a final handshake was made between friends. I was to officially start on Monday morning. I left the office knowing I now had gained the full respect from every employee within the company. I smiled as I walked out onto the street. I was happier than ever, knowing that Vicky and Mike were gone for good. From this moment on, it was goodbye to Doody, and hello to Wonderman.

71

While I was trying to get my life back on a normal track, the Jefferson family insisted on keeping me in the spotlight. Since Matthew Jefferson was known as a prominent Manhattan lawyer, he knew all the right people. With the proper connections, a gala night of dinner and dancing were planned. The date was set for early May and I was to be the guest of honor. Newly appointed Mayor Edward Koch would also be attending to present me with an award for my heroism and a key to the city for my bravery. All in all, I actually was looking forward to this event. Because of all the positive public outpouring bestowed upon me, I didn't feel as shy and awkward in social circumstances as I once was. I had started to turn over a new leaf, and I have to say, I was enjoying it.

72

The event in my honor was more than I could ever have dreamed of. As the guest of honor I was seated among not only Marnie and her parents, but the whole extended Jefferson family. Her two younger sisters, as well as aunts, uncles and grandparents, sat at the first two tables. Our new Mayor of New York, Edward Koch, sat to my right, while Marnie sat to my left. Before the most tasty meal I had eaten in years was served, Mayor Koch made a funny but thoughtful speech on my behalf. As the new mayor of the city, he hoped many others would follow my example, and show bravery when faced with the unspeakable. I was presented with my award and key, and the best night of my life continued. All the while, a full orchestra played music from the Big Band era and couples danced the night away. Twice, I even tested my ballroom dancing skills. Once with the elegant Mrs. Mimi Jefferson, dressed in a stunning blue evening gown, and the other dance with Marnie herself. Sensing I wasn't a dancer by some awkward moves at first, Mimi Jefferson took the lead, allowing me to follow her lead. Marnie, in a yellow evening gown, which accented her blonde hair, danced the waltz with me. As soon as the band started to play, the entire room cleared the dance floor and watched us. As we spun with the grace of Fred and Ginger, a few couples started to clap. Before long, the whole room was applauding louder than ever. Tilting her head back and laughing, she shouted over the noise, "Mr. Jack Rogan, you will always be MY hero! Today, tomorrow and forever." And for the second time, she placed a small peck on my cheek.

As I glanced down into this young angelic face with the big brown eyes, I knew what my purpose had been in life. I was to save this beautiful young girl from her untimely death. She in turn would pursue her law degree, finish top of her class and put bad people away for life. The end of the road for the unjust, and the beginning of a bright future for her.

73

Once again a gallery of photos from the celebration in my honor, had made the all the newspapers. I was a celebrity all over again. For the following few weeks, I was still noticed, pointed out and asked to sign endless autographs and I always obliged. I was getting used to it. People, for the most part, were always polite now. Even younger children and teenagers would shout out Wonderman as I passed. If my life were to continue to carry this name, I guess I would respond to it with a positive attitude.

I had even agreed to appear on one of the major networks to do an exclusive interview. Marnie and her parents also would be present. Having spoken with her father prior to our scheduled appearance, we agreed that any monetary support would be donated to the St. Jude Children's Hospital. A date for our appearance had been set. Once seen on television, my title of Wonderman would be news all over again. I braced myself for the full impact that was due to take place in just three more days. Unfortunately our appearance never made the air. Our spot was replaced by the news about someone more evil than New York had ever seen. My moment in the limelight was over, but this young man's had only just started.

74

His name was Franklin Webb, a drifter, who preyed on older woman. With Cary Grant looks, he was a very handsome man. Some who recalled him said he was a guy's guy and a ladies man. Well dressed and in his late thirties he frequented very upscale restaurants in all the major cities from Los Angeles all the way to the East coast. It is estimated that Franklin killed over forty women in the past twenty years. Having been shuffled from foster care to foster care at birth, he was mentally and physically abused in his early years. Franklin came to despise all women, since he never had maternal love from any of the homes he passed through. Once he turned eighteen and was considered a legal adult, he left Boise, Idaho and headed for the West Coast. Homeless and with no money, he lived off the piers of Santa Monica. It was there that he met forty-two year old Cynthia Welsh. She was left a very wealthy woman from her oil tycoon husband, who was killed in a tragic auto accident, just months prior. Cynthia was a homely woman, with long shaggy dark hair and a crooked nose. Her body however, was knockout material, which is what must have attracted a rich husband to her. She befriended Franklin, one hot sunny afternoon on the pier. Franklin went along for the ride, knowing that this ugly woman found him to be very attractive. She invited him into her home, where he became a permanent guest. For the following six months she wined and dined him, provided he fulfilled her inner desires. Since he had unlimited access to money, he also became addicted to drugs and booze, as such, that she also supplied his habits. Repulsed by this woman, Franklin did what he had to and in time, got used to it. She spoiled him rotten and gave him access to all her accounts. Cynthia was a very lonely and needy woman. Realizing that he could easily swindle her, Franklin started to withdraw larger amounts of cash from her bank accounts to supplement his outside binges. Upon being notified by her bank branch manager of such high dollar withdrawals, Cynthia confronted him. What should have been just a quarrel sorted out by a promise not to take advantage again, turned into a blood fest. Franklin took a butcher knife from the enormous kitchen and severed her head. He cut it off completely and left it on her vanity, for her to stare into her own image for the disgust she brought not only to him, but to the world in which she had existed. Escaping with enough money to last him a while, he left Santa Monica and headed to Los Angeles. Cutting his hair and dying it a different color, he was a new man. Enjoying the wild life by partying at all the hot clubs, he went through the money in no time flat. Searching for his next victim was easy. Franklin targeted middle aged women, who liked much younger men. Landing a second woman of wealth, he followed the same format as he did with Cynthia. Only this time as he continued to steal, he didn't wait to get caught. After he felt he had enough cash to continue his wild drug and alcohol partying spree, he again decapitated his live-in lover. Placing her head in the same fashion as Cynthia on her vanity for all to see, he found this an exhilarating way to depart his victim. It wasn't until after his fourth victim in Dallas, Texas, two years later that the pattern was pieced together, and a serial killer was on the loose. The Vanity Killer was out there and no woman was safe. Each and every time, Franklin changed his appearance and had fooled the authorities time and time again. This murderous spree continued for almost twenty years, until his luck ran out. Franklin Webb, unknowingly picked out his latest would be victim, at a Posh Manhattan restaurant. Lillian Gersh, a multi-millionairess from a pharmaceutical legacy, was also an unattractive woman. Lillian's passion was that she was a true crime story follower. It became a hobby for her. The more gruesome the murder, the more it peaked her interest. Lillian couldn't believe just how many maniacs, prowled the world. Having read an article years ago, that involved a woman named Cynthia Welsh from the West Coast, had left a permanent impression on her. The way the murder was committed by the now known Vanity Killer tortured her inner peace. Over the years, she kept a scrapbook of all the newspaper clippings from each victim's demise. So after nearly twenty years, Lillian knew this deranged man's pattern. So on that very first unlikely night they met, she like all the past victims, was instantly dazzled by this fine suitor, who paid utmost attention to her. Forgetting all about this sick individual, she, like all the others, was swept off her feet. Following the usual pattern that Franklin always had in the past, he again landed a cozy place to shack up. The women he now chose, were much older than the days of Cynthia. Franklin, again would sexually please them, while riding out the storm until that fateful moment when, he would leave his signature mark. Lillian a very sophisticated woman of means, was clueless to her years of following the Vanity Killer's murderous spree. However, what was sure to be her death in the very imminent future, proved futile, when she stumbled upon the album of helpless ladies much like herself. She had come across the scrapbook in her desk, while searching for her will. So taken by this wonderful man that brought her such joy, she was going to change the beneficiary over to Franklin in case of her sudden death. She hadn't glanced at the clippings in quite some time. As soon as she opened the first page, it all hit her. She didn't need to read any further. She was living with the Vanity

Killer and taking care of him. Now believing this was the same man, who had killed so many innocent women over the last two decades, she immediately notified the police. Within twenty four hours, a plan to capture this national notorious villain was put into effect. Lillian was secretly wired as a SWAT team was put in place surrounding the building. FBI agents and NYPD were on hand and staged accordingly throughout the luxurious penthouse apartment, located on ultra-glamorous Fifth Avenue. Giving her best performance, she angrily and repeatedly accused him of stealing money from her. Enraged and ready for the kill, he knocked her to the bedroom floor. As she lay there stunned, he confessed to her that she was like all the others, as he bound her feet and hands with a silk scarf. He then proceeded to the kitchen. While there, he grabbed a butcher knife from a rack and sealed his impending fate. As he went back to finish his work of art, he was swarmed by a dozen of New York's finest. Caught red-handed, they handcuffed him, read him his Miranda rights, and now had enough evidence to put him away for life. Eventually they would seek the death penalty after capturing this cold-blooded killer in the act. Lillian Gersh was noted as being the greatest sleuth of the century not unlike Sherlock Holmes. Lillian, deciding she would take it to her grave, would never admit that if it weren't for her stumbling upon the scrapbook, she would have suffered the same fate as all the others. She basked in her new found fame and glory as headlines across the nation read, **'Vanity Killer now sees his own death in the mirror of a certain sleuth named Lillian.'**

Lillian and Franklin were national headlines and the metro area wouldn't let go of their greatest heroine. With all the attention now on Lillian, Wonderman had taken a back seat. The recent hero in the spotlight only a few shorts weeks ago, was now considered history.

75

Fading into the sunset, I went on to run Wilson Textiles, as if it were my own.

As I was busy running an empire, the entire world was being pulled in all directions. The eighties took over full force. The Pope, closest man to God, had an attempt made on his life. A virus that had never been heard of was killing many homosexual men and was identified as a new plague called AIDS. On a lighter note a video game that became an obsession of millions was Pac-Man. Michael Jackson, lead singer of an all-brother group, went solo and released an album titled, Thriller. A group of walking dead zombies terrorize Michael and his girlfriend in a video. Many people would duplicate the dance around the world. A doll called Cabbage Patch Kid had parents scrambling like mice to find them for holiday gift giving. Astronauts, including a teacher, were aboard a space shuttle named Challenger that exploded during the launch over Florida. This event saddened the entire country for quite some time. Wall Street had all the elements of greed until 'Black Monday' struck, when once again the New York Stock Exchange suffered huge drops. I, for one, feared another Great Depression having lived through one at such a young age. Our company survived. For me, the eighties ended on a sad note. Mr. Roger Wilson, employer and much-loved friend, suddenly suffered a heart attack. The day he passed was a sunny Saturday afternoon on October 14th , 1989. Just two months prior, his wife of fifty-seven years, had died from ovarian cancer after battling it for years. Most of us at Wilson Textiles felt he died from a broken heart. He left it in his will, that his fifty-one percent of shares of the company, were to be left to his only surviving nephew and niece. Since they were only interested in fast cash, they sold them to the only other shareholder with forty-nine percent. Me. I, Jack Rogan Reilly, was now the sole owner of Wilson Textiles.

76

In honor of my dearly departed friend, I kept the company name and ran it as business as usual. Throughout the last ten years I followed the career of a certain young woman, who in fact was making a name for herself. Marnie H. Jefferson was now a well-known prosecution attorney winning more cases than anyone in Manhattan to date. Records showed that more criminals were taken off the streets of New York City and put behind bars than ever. Organized crime families were suffering too as a result of her courtroom appearances. Mostly because of her legal efforts, people were actually starting to feel safe again walking the streets of New York. Proving she was a source not to be reckoned with, she continued to fight for justice for the American people. Married with an infant and another on the way, she strove for a greater position and landed a seat as an honorable Judge to the praise and support of many followers. Throughout her rising career, we kept in touch. Mostly through letters and the once a year Christmas card, Marnie would fill me in on every aspect of her life in great detail, while I chose to keep it simple on my end. In one, she confided in me that she kept her maiden name, since her family tree dated all the way back to Thomas Jefferson. Her husband Andrew wasn't happy at first, but after realizing how the Jefferson name could benefit his loving wife to further her career efforts, he agreed. My letters weren't nearly as interesting. In actuality, my life was very simple. I still led a sheltered life and having just celebrated my sixtieth birthday with my employees, was looking forward to continue working for at least another ten plus years. You see, I really didn't have much, other than my profession. I wasn't looking to give that up just yet. That was until I met a very special lady.

77

You see, as busy as I was running my conglomerate, I still found time for church. I had never forgotten MY walk with Jesus. Some would say I fabricated, others would flat out doubt me, but many would believe and envy my having had the experience. Each Sunday, I attended mass at St. Patrick's Cathedral. Following the mass, I would stay behind and silently say my prayers. I prayed for the continued success of my company, my health and that of all my employees and their families. I even asked the good Lord for world peace, since the unity of our civilization was still unknown. As I finished with all my endless blessings, I was making my way out of the pew, when an older woman blocked my exit by sitting on the end. Excusing myself as I passed her tucked in knees, she looked up. At the same moment we recognized one another after all these years.

"Could it be? Wonderman. I often did wonder, sorry no pun intended what became of you. I had followed your story on rescuing that poor innocent girl from the Coney Island ferris wheel. Then, of course, I got so wrapped up in all my own publicity."

"You're, um excuse me. I remember your name like it was only yesterday. Sleuth . . . ?"

"That's quite all right. Yesterday was over ten years ago. My name is Lillian and it is a pleasure to meet you . . . . ?" She started to laugh herself by continuing, "I guess we're even. Wonderman stuck, but your name seems to have slipped my mind. Oh, wait. It's Jack Reilly, but according to you, most friends call you JR. Whew, I was beginning to think I was getting forgetful. After all, we aren't as young as we were back then. So I'm right, it is Jack?"

For some odd reason, at that moment I felt a connection to this woman. Totally different circumstances threw us both in the limelight, but years later the one common denominator for us both, was our faith. Enjoying the light conversation I said, "Please, call me JR. All my friends do. I guess they didn't nickname you Sleuth Lillian for nothing. Seems you can remember names from years past. Do you come here often?"

Again laughing with the sweetest chuckle she answered, "Why JR, if I didn't know better, I would saying you were flirting with me." Turning more serious she looked over at JR who now stood in the aisle, "Actually, it's the anniversary date of the capture of that monster. God, what a beast he was. I come here to give thanks each and every year on this date. I also pray and hope that the, excuse my language, bastard, will get the death penalty. Seems he is still waiting on death row, while our hard earned tax dollars feed this animal."

"If you don't mind me asking, what do you give thanks for?"

"For being the lucky one. I survived while as many as forty other women didn't. The Lord above must have had a purpose for me. I guess it was to finally put a stop to this madman. Either that, or if I may flirt back, to meet you JR, the infamous Wonderman!"

A purpose. She just said a purpose. All these years and I always had questioned my purpose. How ironic. Something about this woman intrigued me. Although, by her appearance, I could tell she was a couple of years my senior, she acted rather spunky for her age. She made me feel like an old codger, as my mom would say. I liked this lady and didn't want our chance meeting to end here. Instead, I genuflected and whispered in her ear, "If the great Sleuth Lillian would be interested in a man, well let me rephrase that, a wonderman like me, perhaps we could have dinner together. You pick the date and time. Just choose a place where we won't be recognized. On occasion there are still people that will remember one of us as being newsworthy, so I say Oshkosh, to play it safe."

Lillian Gersh laughed out loud. The sweetest chuckle I had heard in years. A chuckle I would want to hear for years to come.

78

Just like that, a relationship blossomed for two senior citizens. Older people need to be loved as much as anyone though some may not believe so. Lillian Gersh was two years short of seventy but didn't look a day older than my sixty years. At five foot four with a full head of white hair, her green eyes still had a sparkle to them. I hadn't weathered all too well, so we looked about the same age. I even had grayish-white hair to cover most of the red that haunted me throughout my life. On our nightly strolls, we walked hand in hand, as young lovers often do. Our love for walking kept us trim, which enabled us to eat as much as we wanted. We often frequented many of the elite restaurants throughout Manhattan. We couldn't spend enough time with one another. As the weeks progressed, so did our feelings for one another. I wanted to spend real quality time with this woman, while we were still young enough to appreciate one another. The only pressure at hand, was the only other thing that mattered to me; Wilson Textiles, the company I now owned. Having built it up to where it was after decades of hard work, the time had finally come. A time I swore wouldn't even be considered, until I was old and decrepit. But the time was finally here, and I had a whole new outlook on life. I found love and nothing was going to get in its way. There weren't enough hours in the day to keep me away from this wonderful woman. But there were too many hours spent at the office limiting my ability to be with her. So with some serious consideration and not too much heavy thought, I came to the conclusion of needing to pack it all in and enjoy our remaining years together. It was time for me to retire.

79

With my decision made, I investigated my best business options and decided to sell. Wilson Textile's was purchased by a Fortune 500 Company, making me a very wealthy man. I gave every employee a huge bonus for their dedicated service. Some would say too generous of a bonus, but they all deserved it. Combined with Lillian's net worth, together we would be considered filthy rich. As we both had more money than we could spend, we decided to send large donations to charitable organizations. I always wanted to help children who suffered from any form of disease, so my contributions were sent to St. Jude Children's Hospital. Marlo Thomas, an actress, producer, and activist, was so pleased with our support of her cause, that we eventually became friends. On several occasions, we could be found dining out with her and husband, Phil Donahue, king of daytime talk shows. Money for us meant more about what we could give rather than what we actually had or needed. So for the beginning of the nineties, we did just that. We donated and shared our wealth with many charities to help the poor and needy, which gave us great pride in our efforts. We even contributed to the World Trade Center fund, which was bombed killing innocent working people and causing some structural damage. One of the victims was a pregnant woman that pulled at New Yorkers' heartstrings in sympathy. The news of the nineties continued. Women no longer let themselves be abused, some were actually fighting back. A woman by the name of Lorena Bobbitt, after claiming her husband had come home drunk and raped her, took brutal revenge. She cut off his penis as he slept, and sped away tossing it out the window, which was later found and surgically reattached. On the scientific front, sheep were being cloned, with talk of humans eventually as well, one day in the very near future. This frightened both Lillian and me. There were enough evil people in this world who didn't need to be duplicated. Not all the news was good. Just two years separating the events, we lost two highly recognizable figures. Princess Diana, ex-wife of Prince Charles, was notably one of the most cherished among women worldwide. She had been killed in a car crash while escaping the paparazzi who chased the car in which she rode through a tunnel in Paris. John F Kennedy Jr., also adored by women worldwide, while piloting a plane to a family wedding in Martha's Vineyard, crashed, killing himself, his wife and her sister. Tabloids like the National Enquirer suffered greatly, since most false news that they reported about both Princess Diana and John F Kennedy Jr., landed them on the cover with records sales for their paper. One sad final note to the spiritual far and near. Mother Theresa passed away within the span of a week after Princess Diana, but was overshadowed by the popularity of the would be queen if she had stayed married to the prince. Lillian and I spent many hours in Church trying to understand the reason all these influential people were passing within such a short timeframe from one another. We never did quite figure out why lives were lost or taken away before their time. However, it did make us realize that life was precious and not to be taken for granted. We would appreciate each and every day while we could. One thing we knew for sure, none of us knows the day or the hour when life ends.

80

While we were enjoying our relationship and love for one another which now marked nine years, Marnie H. Jefferson continued to rise in her political popularity. No longer a criminal judge, she now filled one of the nine seats as Supreme Court Justice.

Nominated by the President and with a majority of the U.S. Senate, she secured her place there. She, as well as her other eight constituents of the Supreme Court interpret the law relative to the United States Constitution. Marnie truly believed in freedom and justice for all, provided the criminally insane were kept behind bars. At the tender age of forty-two, rumors in the political arena circulated that she was considering announcing her run for United States President in the two-thousand presidential election. The country was entering a new millennium and Marnie would not only be one of the youngest presidents to take office, she would be the first female president. A first for our country and hopefully not our last.

81

I still kept my small apartment in Greenwich Village but had years ago moved into Lillian's high-rise apartment on Fifth Avenue. I kept my mine because it was rent stabilized. I didn't want to give it up so that it could quadruple in rent, costing some middle class person an arm and a leg to rent it. Over the last couple of years, I actually placed ads in the classifieds, and sublet it to young eager college students free of charge, while they earned their degrees. One of the recent occupants, who never could have afforded this experience and was eternally grateful, contacted a local radio station about my generosity. I, wanting to remain anonymous to the listening audience, was finally talked into appearing as a featured guest alongside Lillian, for their morning broadcast. Together, our donations to the many charities over the last few years, which amounted to exorbitant contributions, resulted in us being classified as humanitarians. Again, my face was plastered on the front cover of Newsweek. This time Lillian was with me in the cover photo. The headline under our picture now called us superheroes. It read, **'Wonderman and Wonderwoman team up to financially save New Yorkers!'**

82

Once again, we were celebrities wherever we went. Although it wasn't why I did what I did, there was no way to deny it. We had plenty of money and we were willing to share it.

After Newsweek with our cover hit the newsstands, everyone wanted our cash. We were flooded with mail from all over the country asking for all types of monetary support. Organizations, unknown charities and all kinds of religious affiliations from around the world wanted us to send them money. The worst were the letters from everyday hard working people. In the beginning, Lillian and I did pick and choose, and even sent money to the people who had illnesses or were in financial trouble. Our mail tripled when word leaked to the media that we were helping many poor families. We were flooded with letters about mothers, fathers or even their children who were facing terminal illness. It became so disheartening to read that after a while we stopped opening our mail. On the streets where we strolled it was the same. People would run up to us and expect us to give them money. It was not easy at first but we learned to tell them no. In time the begging stopped. On the flip side, there were still many New Yorkers who appreciated what we did, just for the simple fact that it was generous. More often, others simply wanted to say a note of thanks for helping those less fortunate. Having Lillian on my arm, made it a bit more enjoyable this time around.

In either case we had impacted the city in a positive way. How people saw this, whether it be good or bad didn't matter. What did matter, was the person we were about to help next.

83

Marnie H. Jefferson had made her choice. She was announcing her decision to run for the presidency. Tomorrow afternoon would be the big day. Speculation about this event's attendance was that record crowds would turn out.

Having known for the longest time where she would want this to take place, she decided to hold a press conference for all the media as well as her loyal supporters to attend. It was to be held at the Coney Island Amusement Park. When asked why she picked Coney Island of all places, she released a statement. Surprisingly enough she went public about her past, telling all her supporters about her fateful ordeal from long ago. How, when she was still a college student, in the hands of a possessive boyfriend, her life had almost ended. The man known as Wonderman had saved her life. A life that made it possible for her to attain and surpass her goals. A life that would continue to strive for world peace.

84

I was very excited to be part of her first campaign for the presidency. Lillian was just as eager to be in involved. Together we decided we would help fund this upcoming annoucement. Anonymously, we sent a large donation to her campaign fund to sponsor the entire gathering. Along with her parents' contributions for future engagements and other ad campaigns, money would never be a problem. However, after Marnie received the huge endorsement from a small bank in Brooklyn Heights, she did some investigating of her own. Not only was she able to outwit and outsmart most people, Marnie pieced together the trail of paperwork that eventually led back to us.

Taking the time out of her busy day-to-day schedule, Marnie called us up at Lillian's penthouse the day before her long road to the White House was set to begin.

After I answered, I heard a now so familiar voice from all her past television and radio interviews over the years. "Why, JR, if it weren't for the fact that you nearly got yourself killed by pulling a young girl to safety, I might have sent the authorities over to lock YOU up. Just what do you think you're doing? A check in that amount! You do realize that it not only covers this campaign, but with the leftover money, I could pay for Jeffrey and Nicholas' private school tuition straight through to college."

Jeffrey and Nicholas were her two sons who were now ten and eight respectively. Her husband Andrew, more of a stay at home dad, ran a small printing business out of their house. Even though Marnie came from money on her side, it still felt right to help her along by easing the pressure financially should it become necessary as time went by.

Knowing I didn't have much to go on I tried convincing her as I replied, "Honestly, Marnie! Can't a man help out a lady of such stature?" I heard a slight cough from behind me as Lillian made a gesture that she too helped. I jokingly continued, "Um, correction. Can't a man and woman help a lady in distress if they feel like it?"

"Oh, I see how it goes. Now I'm a lady in distress. Before or should I say many years ago, What was I then? A young damsel in distress." I could hear Marnie laughing on the other end.

"Come on, Mrs. President. Can't you please give an old codger a break. I mean I know from all your previous cases that it would be asking for a miracle to have you cut anybody some slack."

"Ok, alright. You win. And what's with the Mrs. President? I didn't even announce my decision and already you have me winning. Honestly, JR. Do you ever quit?"

"No, I don't and nor will you and you know it. So what time are we to arrive tomorrow morning?"

"One of my cars will be there to pick you up at 9:00 am. I go live at noon."

"Pick us up? You don't have to go to all that trouble for us."

"Trouble for you. After all you have just given me. Don't be silly. It is my pleasure."

"Okay, you win. No chance in going against the future Mrs. President of the United States."

"I see that you already assume I will win."

"No assuming on this part. After all, it is what it is."

After a moment of silence on her end, I waited for her to reply.

When she didn't right away I asked, "You did hear me. I said it is what it is."

Sounding like she might have shed a tear by my sincere and persistent belief in her future, she said, "And you JR, are what YOU are. MY hero!"

85

I hadn't slept well last night. I gather it was from all the excitement of the impending day. The young girl, who long ago I alone had saved, would be announcing her run for president. Mrs. Marnie H. Jefferson, the first woman to be president of the United States. The sound of it sent chills down my spine. I couldn't believe we would be on hand, sitting behind her, as she made the announcement on live television and millions of viewers. Thousands of spectators would be at Coney Island Amusement Park too. The thought of returning to the exact spot, where we had met twenty years ago, had the hairs on the back of my neck stand up with anticipation. We had met what seemed like a lifetime ago, through an unfortunate situation at the wonder wheel, but since then established an everlasting friendship. I hadn't been back to Coney Island in so long, that I'd almost forgotten the experiences I had there. There was a time when I couldn't visit there often enough. From the beach, to the piers, to the boardwalk with all the endless rides, games and concessions; Each element held memories of a long ago life.

As I showered and dressed for the big day, Lillian busily prepared a hardy breakfast before we departed for the exciting morning ahead of us. I could sense that Lillian perhaps was just as nervous and excited as I. Lillian looked stunning in a light gray jacket and matching skirt. I, just as dapper in a dark gray three piece suit that matched Lillian's. We both looked debonair. Now, as we waited for the elevator to take us from her penthouse to the lobby of our Fifth Avenue home, we held hands as tightly as we could. We both squeezed one another's hand as if we would never let go. And ironically enough, letting go wasn't an option either of us had in mind.

86

Our car, sent by Marnie, actually turned out to be a black stretch limousine. Marnie wanted to make sure we arrived in style. And arrive in style we did. As we stepped out of our limo, flashes from every angle snapped. Lillian and I hadn't prepared for the onslaught of photographers. It was as if we were on the red carpet for the Oscars. Barricades had been lined up along the boardwalk leading up to the Wonder Wheel. People were pushing up against the wooden planks of the barricade to catch a glimpse of us. Some were shouting, "Look its Wonderman and Wonderwoman!" The crowd would then go wild. News reporters from every major network were present, as were all the top newspaper journalists. What I thought was pandemonium at first was worse, when as we walked along the path, an enormous party bus pulled up. At least a dozen, which I assumed were bodyguards or secret service men, stepped off first. Directly behind were Marnie, her husband Andrew, and their two sons, Jeffrey and Nicholas. Matthew and Mimi, her parents, took the hands of their grandsons. The bodyguards or secret service men surrounded Marnie and her immediate family, as well as another man also in the political circle, and his family too. Close to another thirty to forty family members stepped off the bus. I recognized her two sisters from Christmas pictures sent to me over the years. All Marnie's family, on both sides, were in attendance. Marnie along with her husband and boys were beaming with excitement. The massive crowd of supporters didn't deter the delight etched on their faces. Screams and shouts of approval for Marnie pleased the whole audience of people. Banners, hand-made signs, and American flags waved among the group of dedicated followers. We all were guided to our spots on the stage that had been set up in front of the Wonder Wheel. I was shocked to be led to the front row alongside Marnie. Actually, it was Marnie, Andrew, Jeffrey, Nicholas, her parents, and then me with Lillian. A gentlemen, who was also well known in political circles, sat to her right, with members, I assumed, of his family. The rest of the people sat in the three rows behind us. I couldn't believe the turnout for Marnie. As I had stated to her last night over the phone, everyone was there to welcome Marnie H. Jefferson as our future President. Even someone, who never would have been invited.

87

Roars and applause from the throngs of people were deafening. In just a few short moments, Marnie would step up to the podium and speak about her upcoming campaign to be the next United States of America's President. I couldn't imagine how much louder the noise could get. As I looked around at the crowd, I placed my hand on one of Lillian's knees. I glanced over at her and her face shone with such great love for me. Don't ask me how at that moment I knew it was true love, but I just felt it radiating from her, directly into my heart, since I felt the same way in return. Confirming my last remark, she placed her hand over mine and lightly squeezed it. It was an amazing day all around. For a spring day the temperatures were a cool seventy, with a light breeze off the ocean. With all the body heat generated from the crowd, it felt good. As Marnie was gathering what she needed for her speech, I scanned the mass of people facing us. There were young, old, white, black and just about every other race known to man. Some were actually holding one another's hands as they sang the Star Spangled Banner. It didn't matter what color or ethnic background they were from. They were singing together, as if they were peaceful neighbors, in this diverse crowd. They just held hands and sang. They sang together with such joy and I couldn't think of the right word for what else I was thinking. Looking into their faces you could see hope. Hope for a better world. United as they all stood together in perfect, and then it hit me. Harmony. As if they were all one in Harmony.

88

As Marnie pulled down on the dark blue skirt of her suit, she slowly stood up. It was at that exact moment, as I was still looking over the spectators, that I spotted a man pushing and shoving his way through the people. I assumed that the secret service men, some who had scattered among the audience, would spot this too. It seemed as if everyone was preoccupied with the prospect of Marnie beginning to speak. I should have tried to alert the bodyguards nearest me, but I was deeply fixated on this individual. As he weaseled his way closer, I thought I recognized him from somewhere. I sat up straighter in my chair and pulled my hand out from Lillian's. I continued to focus only on his face to see if I could make the connection. Nothing. I started to break out in a sweat. The man, who was just yards away from the front, had slowed down, so as not to bring any attention to himself. He was dressed in a tan sports jacket and brown khakis. Instead of looking like he was happy to be there, he had a look of purpose written all over his face. And it wasn't a halo over his head either. He looked like a man on a mission. A mission I had hoped would be impossible.

89

Marnie took her last step toward the podium. But instead of going directly behind it, she circled in front and proceeded to take a bow. She wanted to show her gratitude to her future voters. Instead of speaking from the podium, she waved her hands down to quiet the crowd. After what felt like a lifetime, the crowd went silent. Marnie spoke, "Thank you! . . . Thank you! . . . . Thank you all for coming out today to support me. As you all know, I am announcing my run for President. It is official. I, Marnie Harmony Jefferson, would like to be your next President of the United States. Your first WOMAN President!" The crowd went berserk with shouts and applause. Louder than ever. The man, whom I had been absorbed with, reached into his jacket to grab hold of something. As he lifted his arm, a bit of his neck was exposed. Staring back at me was the head of a cobra. Like a ton of bricks, it suddenly hit me. That punk from years ago! Marnie's old boyfriend. Even after all this time, his name came flooding back to me. Kyle! How, why, when, were questions that instantaneously all popped into my head. Now, was not the time to figure this out. I had to act fast. Marnie had just stood up from her last bow, just as Kyle pulled the gun out in full view. He aimed it directly at her chest. People were oblivious to his presence, since they were fascinated by Marnie. Knowing it was now or never, I jumped up. For a man of seventy plus years, oddly enough my legs cooperated. I thanked God for that. A couple of the bodyguards started to move toward me. I now had everyone's full attention. With two giant leaps I landed smack in front of Marnie, who at this point, had a look of utter confusion on her face.

A loud shot rang from below. The crowd so engrossed by Marnie just seconds ago, now started to scatter. In fact scatter was putting it mild, since one young woman screamed "GUN!", mass panic pursued. Three secret service men, faster than the speed of light, jumped on Kyle, knocking him to the ground. Later they would find out that Kyle Adams, the model prisoner, was released only a week earlier, on good behavior. While serving his sentence, he became a born again Christian. He had fooled the parole board into thinking he would go out and preach the good news of the Lord. His determination proved worthy, but his utmost desire was for revenge. To finish what he couldn't from so many years ago. Somehow, the powers that be, failed to inform Marnie of his release. A huge mistake for which prison officials would later pay dearly. For now though, mayhem continued as several people tried to run for cover and safety. Most other people ran for their lives, unbeknownst to them, that I just took a bullet in the heart, and was facing the end of mine.

90

This is what happened next. I DIED! And there you have it my friends. Jack Rogan Reilly, aka JR. and even Howdy Doody, had taken his last breath from this wonderful world, I had finally come to love. Slowly I died, right then and there, in front of the Wonder Wheel at Coney Island. How bittersweet an ending. As I felt the last of the air in my lungs escape, I saw blurry images appear before me. After the lunatic Kyle was fully apprehended and the surrounding area was secured, the bodyguards hovering over and on top of Marnie moved off and away from her. Marnie was the first person hovering within inches of my face. She was sobbing so uncontrollably that tears had fallen onto my cheeks. I could feel the warmth from her tears. She kept repeating over and over, "Not JR! Please God! Not this man! He saved me once before. Oh dear . . . GOD! PLEASEEE . . ." Matthew, her father, and Andrew, her husband, took her by the elbows and lifted her to her feet, so that the paramedics on hand could administer aid. Marnie broke free from their grasp and threw herself on top of me. She knew I wouldn't survive the wound inflicted by the bullet. Turning to face everyone with pleading eyes she begged, "Please . . . . Please . . . ." The saliva was dripping from her lips as she continued, "JR, you old codger. I promise . . . . I . . . won't let you down. By the grace of GOD I will bring the world together. IN perfect harmony. You see . . . ." She leaned in closer as she planted a peck on my cheek and whispered in my ear, "YOU will always be my hero . . . . ALWAYS!" This time she stood up by herself. Slowly I watched her gracefully disappear from my vision and rush into the arms of her awaiting husband. The paramedics, who knew it was too late, still rushed in. I, however, took my last breathe, and rushed out.

91

My body felt unfamiliar, at the moment my eyes had closed for all of eternity. From within my chest, I felt a flutter. Then slowly a ripple began to occur under my ribs.

A part of me had broken off and was leaving my body. A cloud of smoke, almost like a fog or mist, was coming up out of my upper body. As, I lay on the stage in physical form only, the mist slowly lifted up and out of me and started to float upward. I, as well, floated along with it, until I realized what was taking place. I was dead and my soul was departing from the shell of what was once, me. I was ascending at a very slow pace. At a snail crawl, I crept upward toward the heavens. As I was no longer aware of the activity still taking place below, my soul took over from here on.

92

Everything became clear again. I raised my hands to my eyes and rubbed them very hard.

I was my full body again. In the exact dark gray suit I had been shot and killed in. I felt no pain and saw no blood. However, I was standing on clouds that formed an escalator of stairs leading to the heavens. I was glancing in every direction, but all I saw was blue skies. The most astonishing blue I had ever laid eyes on. Powder blue with a touch of turquoise. As I turned to my right again, I almost stumbled backward, certain I would fall all the way back down to earth. There stood Jesus, alongside me, in the same trench coat from all his previous visits. Startled I asked, "So, I died didn't I?"

"Of course you did Jack", Jesus confirmed.

"Am I on my way to heaven?"

"Of course you are Jack", he answered so vaguely again.

"But I have so many questions, unanswered, Jesus!"

Again he replied, "Of course you do Jack."

Before I was just about to ask him to elaborate he said, "Look to your left, Jack and everything you need to know will become clearer, provided you open your heart."

He then pointed past me and I followed with my eyes. Eyes that could now see all that life had to offer.

93

I saw oak trees larger than the Empire State Building. Waterfalls so breathtaking it would leave you speechless. Endless beaches with shores that stretched forever. Lakes so wide, that the naked eye couldn't see the other shore. I wanted to jump off the clouds, of the escalator, to once again, experience what I did from so many years ago. Instead, I observed every glimpse I could absorb, on my ride to my last stop. Heaven.

94

Again, I saw races from every color, living and working hand in hand. There was no racism anymore. The young once again respected their elders. People listened to police officers and respected them too. Couples worked at their relationships. Marriages lasted and divorce was unknown. Cures for all forms of cancer were discovered. Aids stopped killing. Mother Nature worked with us and not against us. Sports figures and Hollywood stars were paid normal salaries in place of astronomical ones. Free healthcare was provided. Big business helped the small ma and pas. Hope was given to the disabled and handicapped. Men held doors for women. Boys helped old women cross streets. Animals that are so wild fed openly, among animals so timid, barely bothering one another. One and every Nation under God, stopped terrorism and lived as a United World in perpetual peace.

95

As my ride to my last stop continued, before I gave thought to what became of Marnie, she appeared everywhere around me. I started to spin in circles soaking in every last detail of her life. She had indeed become the first woman President for the new millennium. She fought long and hard for not just the American people, but for all people. Visiting the world on many tours, people held banners in her honor as she stepped off of Air Force One. Most read 'Power for the people, thanks to Marnie H. Jefferson!' Others read 'Marnie for harmony!' I had to re-read the last few again. 'Marnie for harmony!'

Then it all made sense. Marnie H. Jefferson. She was HARMONY! I looked over at Jesus, who was smiling at my sudden realization.

96

I did have a purpose. My purpose was not only to save this new world leader once, but twice. I sacrificed myself not only for Marnie, but for Marnie to save the entire world.

Marnie was to go on to be not only President of the United States, but for World Leader of all nations for twenty years, elected in part by every living soul. If it wasn't for me saving her back at the Wonder Wheel, our world would have crumbled to ruins. A flash of a poverty stricken world passed before my eyes. What I saw frightened me. Knowing now that my purpose somehow prevented that, brought me my own inner peace. I was meant to save her, as she was to save me. You see, my life prior to Marnie, existed. I existed. But after Marnie, who did indeed bring harmony to this planet, brought me so much more. More than I asked for and more than I needed. I became the owner of a company that became a Fortune 500. I accumulated more wealth than was imaginable. And lastly and most importantly, I found LOVE. Something I had ruled out forever.

97

Panicked about my found love but now since lost, I pleaded to Jesus, "Jesus, please. In all this, I forgot about Lillian. What became of Lillian? My dear sweet Lillian."

I started to cry just imagining what she must have gone through watching me die.

I waited for Jesus to answer. He didn't. I just stood there disbelieving that after my walk with Jesus so many years ago, he would deny me this one last request. The escalator of clouds continued the ascent, and from afar, I noticed what looked like a bright light just ahead. So bright I thought I would need to cover my eyes. It wasn't necessary. My eyes automatically adjusted to the brightness. I needed Jesus to answer me. In fact, I would beg him until he did. Whatever it took, I would do. You see, I was okay with the fact that I died. I accepted my fate. I wasn't okay with not knowing about Lillian. I needed an answer and I needed it NOW.

98

Jesus took my hand before I could even voice my request. As we entered the light, he slowly departed from me. The long black trench coat that he had worn, fell from his back. In its place appeared the most beautiful white robe I had ever laid eyes on. Facing me, he extended his hands out and opened his arms to embrace me. His sparkling blue eyes were an open invitation to share eternity with him. I stepped into the light to walk into his arms.

Just as I was ready to be hugged, I noticed a figure to my left. When I turned, the person came into full view. It was Lillian, in her same light gray skirt and jacket. She looked radiant. She walked over to me and simply but her hand in mine. Without a word exchanged between us, she led the way. Together, we would spend eternity.

99

While I was down on the ground taking my last breath of life, Lillian reacted as any lover would. She stood so quickly to rush into my dying arms. Unfortunately, the shock of the whole ordeal, had been too much for her. Before she even took her first step, she grabbed her chest, tumbled over, and collapsed. Having been eight years my senior added additional stress to her stability. The trauma and thought of losing her greatest love was too heavy for her heart. She suffered a fatal heart attack and she died before I did. SHE waited for me. So, as we made our way into the light, we were greeted by all our loved ones, who had gone before us. It really is what you are led to believe through your faith. The white light and all your loved ones, really will be there with open arms. As was Jesus, whom I had once walked with.

100

After all, Jack Rogan Reilly, had really LIVED.

This is an enthralling sixth novel for **Vincent N. Scialo**. Unlike his previous five novels, this is his first attempt at a spiritual story that draws the reader into the possibility of what ifs. His first novel The Rocking Chair still receives much acclaim since its publication nine years ago. The sequel *Randolph's Tale (A Journey for Love)* has readers not wanting to put it down. Both these novels are still talked about amongst many book clubs today. For those who crave the ultimate in horror and suspense, a taste of *Deep in the Woods* will leave you speechless. This novel is sure to keep you up late at night with the lights on. And if you ever wondered what lives the seven little men led before meeting the purest of snow, Vincent offers a dark fabled fairytale. *Heigh-Ho* is for the young at heart still in love with classic bed-time stories. *Not by Choice* will grip you from start to finish as this medical suspense has the reader rooting for the main character throughout the story. Vincent continues to perfect his work while residing in Bellmore, Long Island, with his wife Jennifer and two children.